HOW TO STOP YELLING AT YOUR KIDS

A POSITIVE PARENTING APPROACH FOR DEALING WITH DIFFICULT CHILDREN TO CREATE A STRESS-FREE ENVIRONEMENT

JAMIE WILLIAMS

OAKRIDGE PRESS

CONTENTS

PREFACE

I think you have heard the saying, "It's not all sunshine and roses" (Main, 2013), which you can apply to parenting too. Some parents are very selfish with their children because they are too attached and controlling. Helena is one of them, whose mother was overbearing from infancy and whose daughter's crying irritated her. She lost her vision at seven years old but got it back after 24 surgeries. Her mother, Maurine, was unconcerned about her daughter's health problems and manipulative, and she frequently pretended to be ill to get attention.

Her father was also a narcissist, a gambler, and an alcoholic who was aware of his ex-wife's behavior and tried to confront and protect Helen. However, her grandparents, who were supportive and did not blame their granddaughter for her mother's problems, helped her grow up as a healthy individual. Nowadays, Helen and her mother's relationship is still emotionally distant, and Maurine thinks she is the center of attention but keeps in touch.

A famous Arabic poet and philosopher, Khalil Gibran, stressed that you are not the owner of your children because they can make decisions for themselves. They owe you nothing, even though you gave birth to them, took care of them, and raised them. Remember that it is not a merit to have children but a gift to you, and you can learn from them as they grow up because life is not standing still. Punishment and manipulation of children can only cause psychological harm when they do not meet your expectations and they start to resist and fight against you.

The only things you can give them are unconditional love and support. You might also give them the freedom to feel, create, and just be happy. That's all. Children only need the opportunity to grow up as fully functioning individuals and go in the desired direction with suitable means. This will help them feel like they are brave, valuable, and important members of their family and society.

Yes, as a parent or guardian, you can have a consistent and happy relationship with your children, even when expected challenges arise. You just need to be more considerate and implement the right strategies. Therefore, you need to be open and honest, be more demanding of yourself, and respond appropriately to the growth and development challenges of your children. Simply begin to see your children as they are — their needs and abilities, what they say, and how they feel. It will help to keep a healthy relationship with them.

This book, How to Stop Yelling at Your Kids, will teach

you how to parent your children with the objective of establishing healthy relationships. It will offer you useful strategies to deal with your children if they display difficult behavior. Moreover, you will gain an understanding of the challenges that can develop between narcissistic parents and their children. Furthermore, you will realize that there are many other parents who face similar challenges when raising their children. However, most importantly, you will understand the importance of having the "right approach" when dealing with children who display difficult behavior to maintain their overall well-being.

1

WHAT NARCISSISTIC PARENTING LOOKS LIKE

Parents with narcissistic traits face a unique set of challenges when raising children, often stressing their authority and misusing it. Therefore, if children face challenges later in adult life, the reason might be how their parents raised them.

What Is Narcissism?

In simple terms, narcissism itself is a psychological state when people think that they stand out from ordinary people and are very important, which irritates those around them. Others may find them attractive at first because they appear very confident, even though they are not. It is true that the number of such people is increasing nowadays; however, there is no psychological research evidence. For example, people who are constantly taking selfies of themselves or famous people who show their personal lives to the world. This kind of behavior can become an obsession and disturb normal life.

When you are narcissistic, you might feel the desire to be appreciated, admired, and noticed to feel happy. It may cause harm to your interpersonal and work relationships because you are not easily satisfied and not willing to change your behavior easily, and it becomes hard for others to be around you. It is especially hard for narcissists, who look very pleasant and attractive at first, to truly love someone long-term, be honest, and treat another person equally because they lack understanding of emotions. Moreover, narcissistic people are very strict when it comes to romantic relationships, and they are selfish because they want what those people have for themselves and want to separate from family and friends.

Nevertheless, based on the study, people who suffer from a high level of narcissistic personality disorder (NPD), which is not common, are well aware of being selfish (Psychology Today Staff, 2019). It means they do not truly appreciate themselves, but are so in love with their ideal selves that they hide their insecurities behind masks. But, in the absence of such disorder, people can, from time to time, be selfish, unpleasant, and preoccupied. Besides, people are usually diagnosed with depression or other mental disorders other than NPD.

The problem of narcissism is by no means a new phenomenon, and it has become a frequent diagnosis and the focus of attention among psychologists. In 1979, Robert Raskin and Calvin S. Hall created the widely accepted Narcissistic Personality Inventory (NPI) method, which is very useful to determine whether a person deals with a narcissistic psychological disorder and what the reasons are. The scoring varies from 0 to 40, and usually, the result is somewhere in the middle, although some people reach high points. For example, if you have higher scores, at first glance you might be considered a very charismatic person, but in reality, you are overly proud of yourself and deal with difficult emotional issues in spite of the fact that you are still a healthy person (Psychology Today Staff, 2019).

How do you know if you are narcissistic? Sometimes people can simply ask, "Do you think you are narcissistic?" and your answer can be "yes," but at other times, you might not know this but have specific traits. You might find it difficult to accept criticism, and you are very vulnerable to it; therefore, you become impatient, angry, and easily insulted, and your mood changes frequently. Moreover, when you have this disorder, you view yourself differently than others, and you might not think that there is anything wrong with that. For example, you

- Think that you are better than others.

- Live in an imaginative world to feel more successful, powerful, and beautiful.

- Must constantly have someone admire you to boost your ego.

- Show envy and are jealous of others.

- Think that you have the right to obtain what you desire, e.g., luxury cars.

Moreover, how do you view the world? You

- Can't empathize with other people's feelings.

- Use other people without shame and treat them as objects.

- Do not think about the effect of your behavior on others.

- Concentrate only on your own needs.

- Threaten people who are weaker than you.

However, it is still possible to change a situation with the help of specialists, for example, a psychotherapist. Ideally, it would be great if you sought professional help when you noticed that you had some narcissistic traits, and you might find out that you did not necessarily have NPD. It would boost your self-esteem, make you less vulnerable to emotional harm, make you happier with your life, and improve relationships. You would be able to recognize things that were untrue, understand narcissism itself, and experience reality subjectively.

Challenges of a Narcissistic Parent

It is important to mention that narcissists, because of the nature of their condition, often have trouble forming and maintaining relationships because their view of themselves and others is distorted. They are only able to communicate with people who are similar to them, not average, and it causes some challenges when raising children. Consequently, life with such parents is very hard, and their children find it difficult to believe that others can have deep connections with their parents and be happy with their lives. The problem is that narcissistic parents think a lot about their own well-being and feel more important, so others must give them what they need. They might also

- Want special treatment.

- Think that their needs are more important than those of their children.

- Be manipulative and controlling.

- Do not avoid shouting.

- Can accuse children of doing something they did not do; for example, their father may not want to come home on time due to a mess at home, such as toys strewn about.

As a result, their distinctive characteristics of behavior make it harder to maintain healthy relationships with their children. First, they require a lot from their children, lack empathy, and express constant disapproval. Second, they also refuse to accept responsibility for their mistakes and instead blame others. Their children never satisfy them with what they do or choose and get a lot of criticism, making them feel stupid. Additionally, they find it hard to express their emotions, create a negative self-image, and, when criticized, react very violently.

Another problem is that such parents do not forget to talk about their successes when raising their children in order to get praise. They emphasize that they love their children very much, care a lot about them, and gave up a lot for their sake. However, the most important aspect is that they are not tolerant of anything that disagrees with their principles, views, and needs. This is because they see their children as their continuation, who should act the same. In the best possible way, children are free to express themselves as individuals, which helps them become confident about their abilities and be emotionally stable as adults, but not when their parents are narcissists. Usually, they want their children to fulfill dreams that they were not able to do, such as:

- Studying a particular profession.

- Playing an instrument.

- Wearing clothes they wanted to wear as a child.

They also want their children to act as if their lives are perfect and not show weakness to others outside the home. It makes it hard to be genuine. However, they might not want their children to be better than them too. For example, a mother would cut her daughter's hair so as not to look prettier than her when she gets compliments about that.

Later, when children are fully grown, they become anxious and unable to make life decisions for themselves because they are eager to please others. Especially in romantic relationships, where they feel a constant need to sacrifice a lot. They have low self-perception, and this is because they learned not to show that they are not sure about something and feel insecure. Moreover, as adults, they feel inadequate and judge themselves because they strive to be perfect, as they needed to be as children in front of their parents, and maintain that image, which is unrealistic.

When children are still small, they do not understand that their parents have narcissistic traits. However, when they reach the age of 12 and start to think critically, they begin to interact more with their peers, who have a lot of influence on their development, and start to want to be more independent. In this case, they might want to leave an impression on their friends and would not want them to spend time alone because they demand their children's attention. For example, their parents may begin to manipulate them and make them feel guilty by claiming that they no longer understand them because they spend less time at home. It is not easy for parents to accept that their children are growing up and want to form closer relationships with others. This makes it hard to have real friends or any friends at all.

Teenagers might notice that their parents make mistakes with their decisions, but instead of accepting the fact, they become angry and impose penalties for noticing that. Their children might see them as not being perfect and having addictions such as drinking alcohol or simply weeping for some reason. Therefore, for example, narcissistic parents

- become cold and avoid attachment.

- unexpectedly say that they do not have money for the school trip, though they do.

- do not give an expensive gift if children do not do what they are expected to do.

This is a critical time in children's lives when they most need to be loved, cared for, and given advice and assistance. If that is not the case, it becomes hard for them when they grow up and form interdependent relationships with other people. Therefore, as adults, they are likely to not communicate effectively or suffer from domestic abuse because they are in relationships where they have to "work" for love and do what others want to get approval. To prove that fact, a study published in the International Journal of Psychology and Psychological Therapy included 400 participants in their early 20s. It showed that growing up in a family with narcissistic parents is the cause of their current mental issues with depression and anxiety (M. Darcy, 2020).

Narcissism is not only an irritating personality trait when people are very self-centered, but it can be a serious personality disorder. Moreover, it is not always easy to recognize such people. Factors of genetic or environmental origin might be the cause of this disorder, and the help of specialists might be necessary. Parenting is a very important role and a tendency toward narcissism can cause psychological damage to children when they grow up. However, when they become adults, they should define the limits of communication with abusive parents and make it clear how they want to be treated to make it possible to communicate.

2

THE WORLD'S HARDEST JOB

It does not matter whether you are a narcissistic parent or guardian or not; parenting is challenging, but you must remember that your child depends on you to nurture, protect, and guide them from their birth until they are fully grown and become independent. It plays a crucial role in the development of children's social, psychological, and emotional well-being. Being a parent is not always easy, and some children, especially adolescents, are more difficult than others. If those needs aren't met, it can have long-term negative consequences, such as:

- Making them consider themselves as victims.

- Causing problems with personal identity.

- Finding it hard to set emotional and personal boundaries.

Therefore, taking care and supporting children through their development is much more important than just feeling a biological connection because it helps them better-overcome difficulties in life and be successful.

Parenting Is Difficult

Parenting has a lot of influence on children's lives. Parents should keep in mind that children are born with their individual characters, traits of mind and behavior, and objects they want to reach. Yes, we live in a modern world where everything is changing like crazy, but still, children need to get the same things from their parents, such as:

- feeling safe

- understanding limits and boundaries

- being supported

- being loved

To have happy children and a strong emotional bond with their parents, parenting should be balanced, not too strict or neglectful. However, there are general and common challenges to parenting that make it a hard job. One of the challenges is balancing one's family and career.

Previously, mothers were those who raised and took care of their children, while fathers earned money for the family and had decision-making power. Nowadays, as times have changed, both parents are equally important and play the same roles. In comparison to previous generations, fathers became more involved in child-rearing; for example, they helped to build necessary skills, train talents, and shape their behavior. Though mothers work and have careers, they give enough time, love, and attention to their children and help them grow healthy.

Another challenge is financial stability at home; having a lot of money is not the case, but living a comfortable life is. It means having a safe home to live in, clothes to put on, and to fulfill other basic needs, which parents must ensure. Let's not forget about the importance of receiving a qualitative education and meeting parents' values, which means creating a healthy environment to grow up in. The school gives a proper education to a child, but a parent must contribute too. It can be done through reading and doing homework together, they

- Show their children how to properly behave.

- Encourage them to be interested in learning.

- Help develop curiosity.

Participating actively in their learning process, and thus being good parents, is critical for children's development. A study by the Child and Family Research Partnership (2017) group shows that when fathers act like guides, it has a greater effect than getting instructions from a teacher. For example, children are expected to get the highest results more frequently (39% more), not be kept in the same grade (45% less), or have less of a chance to have children in adolescence (75% less) (J. Peterson, 2022).

Similarly, it is important to protect the physical and emotional health of children. Good parents should regularly take their children to the doctor to be sure that their overall health is in good condition. Moreover, when children feel loved, it helps them grow, develop, and be emotionally stable. Having fun with their family and receiving physical touch such as hugs and kisses makes them happy. Nonetheless, there is a lot of information that pulls parents in different directions because each child's needs are unique, and good parents can support them with the right techniques. They can simply

- Observe how others act and try to imitate it.

- Experience.

- Change actions if something goes wrong.

Please note that daughters and sons could have different needs from their mothers and fathers. Moreover, not all children live with both parents, even biological ones, which do not make their relationship less fulfilling. To solve problems that arise, parents can sometimes simply trust their instincts and act accordingly.

One of the real-life examples is Miguel and his nine-year-old daughter, Dylan. He grew up without a dad who would give advice, so he solved problems himself. Dylan became an adult, and his girlfriend got pregnant, which made him wonder, "What is it like to be a dad?" Using his judgment, he decided to fully participate in the nurturing of his daughter and gave her a lot of attention as an expression of love.

Now Dylan is like a best friend to him. They do things together like go to movies, ride bikes, or run in the park. He admits that he is afraid of her growing up and becoming less attached to him, but he is looking forward to her becoming a more independent and great person. Even though Miguel did not know what it was like to have a father, he did not neglect his daughter because he had a parental instinct, which helped him make the right decision.

Another example is Diane, a mother, and Stefen, who struggled with gender identity. The year 2017 was very devastating for them and Stefen's sister because their husband and father died. Stefen admitted to his mother that he was a transgender, and she agreed to have surgery and legally change documents. Diane was terrified of losing her child after the death of her husband, who would have been supportive and allowed his child to truly be himself. Stefen credits his mother's support for allowing him to persevere during his transition.

Two completely different stories show how it is important to get love and support from parents to be happy and live a fulfilling life. Moreover, to create strong bonds, it is important to listen, not judge, and respect other people and their decisions.

Difficult Circumstances

Not only parents but also children may also face their own emotional, physical, and mental challenges that require additional attention and consideration from them. Some children have an unusually high level of energy in comparison to others because they behave violently at home and at school. Yet, it might be difficult to determine whether a child just behaves badly or whether there is a neurological condition that provokes such behavior. There might be many reasons why children are anxious and hard to calm down:

- Many activities during the day can make children hyperactive.

- They find it challenging to express strong emotions.

- Children can feel eager to play because they have not engaged in any activity for too long.

In that case, the evaluation of a specialist might be required if that happens quite often, and punishment should be avoided. Various types of neurological conditions can affect children and their behavior, and one of them is autism. Rachel is a mother of two children with completely different temperaments and personalities. She has tasks every day: not to become crazy, trust in herself when raising children, and find balance by giving enough attention to both of them. Her daughter is a calm child, while her son suffers from ADHD and hyperactivity, plus autism disorders.

At first, it wasn't easy to understand why her brother got more attention than her, so Rachel decided to take them out together more often and let her daughter choose activities they would engage in. Eventually, their connection became stronger as they grew up. Although Rachel never told her children that one was easy and the other was hard to handle, her daughter understands that her brother has special needs. One of the challenges is finding a compromise because her son is not willing to do some things like dress up and have social anxiety in a place full of people. She let him choose to wear a soft cotton polo shirt to feel more comfortable, and then he agreed to go to the concert.

When parenting a child with autism, parents should remember that their child's behavior is due to the diagnosis and not lose their cool at difficult times. However, research shows that having a structured and consistent parenting style is the most effective way to parent an autistic child who experiences a lot of negative emotions (O'Connor, 2022). For example, Rachel's son wants to be loved and cared for when he has difficulties and asks to be hugged. No matter how difficult a child's behavior can be, they are able to recover quickly and love their parents. Having two different temperamental children can be an advantage because parents become more empathic, patient, and supportive of others who have similar children.

One more disorder that affects children is attention deficit hyperactivity disorder (ADHD). Those children have such qualities as:

- Creativeness.

- High emotional sensitivity.

- Reduced ability to learn and engage in everyday activities.

- Having an affective disorder.

Sometimes there can be no symptoms at all, but making a plan for families who have children with ADHD is necessary. Those children cause a lot of trouble, seek attention, and have strong personalities. When they grow up, they can become artists who are loners with great imaginations. In addition, children might just be very active. There is nothing to worry about, and this can lead to great success in the future, assuming it is not a disease. However, if it is, life can be very hard for them, and they can start doubting themselves, punishing someone, or avoiding others in subtle ways. If you have a child with ADHD, they can adapt to their surroundings, but you should take these steps:

- Admit the truth about the way your child is, even if you do not understand why.

- Agree that your and your child's personalities are different and you can be distant.

- Find something or someone that can calm down your child, such as a friend.

- Talk to your child about their concerns to make them feel less lonely and emotionally controlled.

- Accept that your child's behavior is unique, and that it is acceptable for them to behave differently than others.

- Reward acceptable behavior with something, such as a car ride. When they do what they like, it can help to strengthen their identity.

- Give them an opportunity at home to express themselves properly, such as through conversations.

However, difficult children may face challenges with anxiety and anxiety disorders, among other behavioral issues. Anxiety may occur in different situations, and calming down may not help. For example, in a doctor's room, during a party held for a friend's birthday, or in extreme weather conditions. Mindful techniques such as taking deep breaths or finding something fun in a situation that causes stress.

Agoraphobia is one of the anxiety disorders that children may face. For example, Jen has five daughters, but the youngest of them, Emma, experiences anxiety when leaving the house. A mother's task is not to show irritation that one of her daughters fails to keep up with her sisters. Instead, she tells her other girls to be patient and give themselves several minutes to calm down and get ready. It is good for a parent not to show signs of being anxious but to be understanding and supportive to avoid more unpleasant reactions from such a child.

Children with ADHD, including autism, may also be predisposed to depression. It might be difficult to recognize its symptoms since children do not talk about them. Your job is to create a comfortable home environment where your child is not afraid to talk about anything, including depression, which does not go away on its own. One study shows that if parents do not respond to the mood changes and irritation of a child, behavioral problems will grow and their relationship will become difficult (Stormshak et al., 2000).

They Rely on You

Parents and children may face their own set of challenges, but the responsibility of managing difficult situations for children with autism and ADHD is ultimately the parents'. It is very true to say that it is harder to control emotions for highly sensitive children and they take things personally. So, in what ways can you help them deal with hard emotions?

- Create a safe and peaceful environment at home in a particular place, which would help to combat your own emotions.

- Consider your child's strengths while accepting the difficulties that may arise.

- Discover what causes your child to react violently and devise appropriate responses.

If your child is very young, their emotions can shift quickly, catching you off guard and making you feel helpless. Because they lack such ability, you as a parent can assist your child in gaining practice managing those emotions. It will help a child become more confident in their abilities. It is important to teach a child not to hide and refuse to admit negative emotions, but to determine them and speak about them. Strive to do your best to ensure that your child gets the best possible chance at a comfortable life. It would be good to give your child direct and clear instructions, which would help to reduce difficult behavior, and consequently, they

- Will better hear you.

- Do what they need to do.

- Reply to questions.

To avoid crying when a child is occupied with something like playing, you can remind them how much time is left for eating dinner, for example. In addition, you can also talk about that activity with your child or join, which would prevent resistance and develop their ability to manage social and interpersonal relationships well. Moreover, if you want your child to be better at controlling themselves and more confident as they grow up, let them make their own schedule. Define options that your child would be able to choose, for example, taking a shower either before or after dinner.

Difficult children do not always behave the way they should, so be consistent and not give attention to a child for a short period of time when they misbehave until they cool down, but they must know what negative behavior can result in a time-out. For example, if the reason was not completing the task, once a child is calm, they should be told to complete it, and it won't let them escape from an unpleasant situation until it is resolved.

Parenting a difficult child who has not just bad behavior but an illness may be challenging and tiring. However, selecting the appropriate steps can make the process easier and help develop the necessary skills. For you as a parent, it is important not only to meet their survival needs. Being a consistent, patient, supportive, and active listener can help a child gain confidence and avoid emotional outbursts and inappropriate behavior. The best thing for you, as a parent of a difficult child, would be to learn not to be anxious because your child is different and not to show it to them so they don't feel differentiated.

3

PAVING A
PATH FOR SUCCESS

A stress-free environment is a goal of parents who have to raise children with difficult behavior, and to reach it, they must be aware of their shortcomings, collect necessary resources, and adjust their mindset to move forward.

Be Aware of Your Reality

Accepting reality can be quite a challenge, but you have to do it if you want to reach your intended goal of raising your children correctly. You should understand the way they are, not how you want them to be, and that will help reduce the effect of distress. Moreover, when you become aware, you know what to do to maintain healthy relationships with your children. Yes, it's really possible, and you can really change something about the situation, but if you disapprove of the reality that you are a parent with narcissistic traits or that your child is different, which makes parenting difficult, it will add more pain and suffering.

So how can we better solve everyday problems with parenting and move forward in the right direction? You should learn not to see only the good and bad in your relationship. You can become aware of the problem when you perceive it, and then it will help you solve it. Increasing your awareness may allow you to see problems more clearly than you previously thought, and you will be able to recognize things that divert your attention.

Remember that you and your child may have different perceptions because your awareness is different, which is normal. Therefore, your goal is your family, and learning how to be a better parent with a shift of attitude and utilizing life resources can assist you in becoming one. When seeking this goal, do not do it only because of others, though you may consider them too. Do not try to please anyone, not even your family members; be honest with yourself. A goal itself shouldn't be too difficult to reach because you must take other difficulties that may occur and skills you need to develop into consideration.

Life resources, which can come up as answers, strategies, solutions, and ideas, are necessary to work through challenges and achieve your goal, and the best of all is that you can develop your own too. They can be external (aside from you), such as:

- Books

- Weblogs

- help from other people

And eternal (within you), such as your

- Knowledge

- Behavior patterns

- Operation or general abilities

- Self-management solutions

First, it is important to determine what resources you already have and what you need to develop with the necessary actions. If it is something that you have never experienced before, it may make you feel worried. Perhaps you don't know how to act, what the starting point is, or what to do to achieve it. To be more confident and assured, you can make a list of life resources, and they will help you make a plan of what to do. In order to achieve a goal and solve a problem, you must first determine what keeps you from it, and you can ask yourself:

- What resources do I already have?

- Are they acceptable, or will I need to add more?

- What resources do I need to obtain?

- How do I obtain them?

Your chances of reaching your goal get bigger when you have more things on your list of life resources, but what's important is how you use them and whether they can give you an answer to your question. You can use many different life resources to achieve a goal and solve problems, and one of them is a mindset, which can include:

- Personal characteristics (what are they? Do they help me?)

- Language (e.g.: what questions, assertions, words evoking emotional response, and quotes inspire, guide, help make progress, and give the power to achieve something?)

- Stimulus (what mental stimulation have I created?)

- Beliefs (my own, others', and lives: what powerful beliefs do I have?)

Moreover, make your goal a positive statement from the very beginning to pave the way for success and inspire you; for example, "Do it perfectly," but don't say, "It's too difficult to do; don't even try." You will have to be patient because it takes approximately 66 days to develop new patterns of mindset based on the survey (Greene, 2020). Over time, it will become a natural habit to think positively, and you will be able to find positive aspects in any negative situation. As you become more aware, you will improve the quality of your life.

Acquire Your Tools

When you seek to reach your goals, you should realize the situation and consider the importance of doing your homework. It is to ensure the availability of the required tools and resources to achieve your goals. If you admit to being a narcissistic parent, you will need a different set of resources to overcome the damaging effects of narcissism. You may also require greater support to ensure you are on track.

Start collecting the necessary information. It is a good thing if you already have some knowledge and past experiences that can help you adopt appropriate responses to present conditions. Be sure that you have enough information about the present situation. It will be helpful to decide how to solve problems because collecting information is the biggest part of critical thinking.

You may begin asking yourself what sources to look at because there are tons of them, but not all the information is right, and you seek to find it. Just ask yourself simple questions starting, for example, with "when," "why," or "what" to gain information. It will assist you in sorting out what information is useful and what is not. After you've identified your questions, look for sources that can provide answers; you can start with the library's catalog system. Organizations and groups may be another option, as well as a department at the place where you work that has some information on your topic.

Relying on guides and reference books is not a bad thing, but be careful because there is much more information than necessary. Nevertheless, if you do, you don't have to read the whole book; just look at

- The table of contents

- Index

- Headings or chapter titles

You can find an index page in some reference books, which is near the end of the book. It can be a very useful tool for you because it gives more information than the table of contents, including page numbers on your topic. A table of contents or index is not necessarily a part of every book; instead, you read the headings or chapter titles.

As is usual, you can search for information on the internet too, but make sure the sources are trustworthy and the information is correct:

- Enter your topic's keywords to get a list of websites.

- Click on those that are relevant to you.

- Look for answers to your questions on each of them.

Remember what you already know and have experienced while looking for information on the internet, because during your life you have gained a lot of valuable information on different topics. For example, perhaps you saw a TV show discussing your problem. It will help faster to find a solution, make a decision, and reach a conclusion. Don't forget to look for information from various sources!

Yet you might think that a book you found can answer all the questions, but another one can have new and additional information. The key is to find the best and most reliable sources and select all the necessary information from them. Parents who have trouble with narcissism should have access to the right resources. This book, How to Stop Yelling at Your Kids, is a perfect example of a narcissistic parent willing to acquire the right tools.

Develop the Right Mindset

The right mind is necessary for you to achieve something successfully. Examine your approach to parenting to ensure that you are not doing it from a pessimistic, resistant, and hopeless point of view, as this will ultimately affect your success rate. You can ask yourself if those negative thoughts are reasonable and true. How effective will they be after some time? Relax and don't be too critical of yourself because everyone makes mistakes, and it really does not mean that you are unsatisfactory.

If you made a mistake, think about it as a lesson that will help you grow and improve. Maybe you won't be able to change some things, but other things that you can change will require action, so simply accept it. In order to make changes whenever they are possible, you will have to discover the real you and your fears. Moreover, you will examine your own thoughts and compete with them to bring happiness into your life.

Thus, if you catch yourself struggling with the right mindset, there are tips and strategies on how you can improve your approach to parenting. The more often you practice, the faster you will see more positivity in your life. Please note positivity is much more than when you are pleasantly bright and have a smile on your face; it is how you perceive your life and look at the bright sight of it. However, where do you begin? Here are some of the steps:

•	Think about your strengths in your relationships with your family that have helped you in the past at difficult times.

•	Meditate, and it will help you get rid of negative thoughts.

•	Change your thoughts when you have too many negative ones.

Do you want a long-lasting effect? Practice a positive mindset yourself by expressing gratitude for everything good in your life, which, for the best possible effect, you should do without interruption. Start doing it and writing in a gratitude journal about, for example, why you are thankful for your family. You can write about it in about two weeks, and when they are over, write about another thing. Do it slowly without rushing and spend about 10–20 minutes every day, and you will see how your attitude is changing and you are starting to see things that you hadn't noticed before but already were. Your children can also do this practice in their journal of gratitude for the things that they are grateful for.

Additionally, you can try to practice gratitude with your children, not in journal form but by using "stones of gratitude," which they will find fun and interesting and can do every day. What is necessary to begin? Just find small, regular stones and paint a heart on them, not in journal form but by using "stones of gratitude," and they can do it every day.

You may also keep a positive journal, which is analogous to a gratitude journal and can improve your mindset. By using it, you will be able to identify what's good about the day that happened, even the smallest things, and write down at least three things; do it for the whole week. Besides, if you want to, you can keep one journal for several purposes. One part would be for gratitude and another for positivity, but on different pages. Your child can also try another similar technique and create an "Awe journal," where they can write about what's nice, unusual, wonderful, and good that happened that day.

However, bad things may happen, and you may need to stop paying attention to them with the help of positive self-talk, which could be very helpful in the future to deal with stressful experiences. You can list some positive statements in your worksheet but also on small cards of paper for notes that you can carry with you; for example, "I don't feel okay and I can make the right decision to stop it" or "All of this is because of what I experienced in the past, but now everything is alright."

The great news is that you can help your child practice a positive mindset and teach them to look optimistically at themselves, situations, and communications through activities. For example,

•	Teach them to act kindly to understand its importance, such as by helping an elderly neighbor with routine tasks at home or a friend with their homework.

•	Share something positive with your child about what happened to you, which will make you laugh and hold each other close; it will help to strengthen your bond.

•	Offer your child the chance to practice loving-kindness meditation by using four phrases aimed at someone they love, such as "Be happy. Be safe. Be healthy. Live without problems."

•	If you have a teen, make the transition easier by encouraging them to use positive affirmations such as "I am generous" or "I am good the way I am."

The whole family can cultivate positive thinking through activities. For instance,

•	Try to express your feelings for your child in writing. Then they can read those letters in the morning and begin the day in a great way. Accordingly, they can do the same for their siblings.

•	Help your child to create a collage on the board with pictures or texts that symbolize their dreams, desires, ambitions, and aims.

•	Let each family member create a "silky character trait person" on the paper and then try to determine what positive personal attributes each of them has and write about them.

- Engage with your child in a "success of the day" activity where you talk about what good happened on the day, for example, you finished a project. Your child can record in a journal about their accomplishments to be inspired.

Developing a positive mindset through worksheets or different activities can be a very helpful technique for you, as a parent, and your children. Being optimistic is not only advantageous because you become more optimistic, self-aware, and resilient, but you will also have better health, be better able to adjust to stressors, and feel less depressed. However, a positive mindset doesn't mean being positive all the time, seeing the positive in every situation, and being always successful. It means that you accept both positive and negative things but remain optimistic.

In order to become successful at parenting, you must acknowledge all of your failures and reach out to various sources that can help you analyze, take the right steps, and solve this problem. With tips and strategies for yourself and your entire family, you will be able to develop the right mindset and change past habits over time.

4

LISTENING TO EFFECTIVELY COMMUNICATE

You, as a parent, must be willing to listen and communicate in the best way you understand how to raise a child in the best possible way. The words that you say and your behavior are equally important in communication, which sends a message to your child.

To Be Heard

So, what does it mean to be a good parent? It's when you are an active listener and take into consideration your child's needs, joys, sadness, and perspective on life, and it is a skill that you can easily develop over time. To grow psychologically healthy, a child requires two basic things from their parents: recognition and approval. If you fail to do it, the consequence can be damage to their self-confidence, and they will have to deal with it as adults.

All your growing child wants is that you hear him, and this way you can have better communication without disagreements happening all the time. For example, you may tell your child, if you have a teenager, not to smoke, and they act as if they do not understand what you are saying. Commanding your child to stop doing something will not help or change their behavior unless you offer them alternatives that will bring them happiness, such as:

- Music

- Sports

- Art

- Relationships

They probably do as their friends do or want to look more mature. Further, there can be many other reasons why your child has those cigarettes, so act healthy and ask about them. Show that your child is important to you; let them express their feelings. Reflect on them as much as you can because if you bring this issue up a lot, they will find it difficult to interact directly and turn inward.

Don't overreact because you are angry and annoyed by the unpleasant situation that occurred, and your child may not forget what you said and not react to your questions in the future. It's no good to show that you can't control yourself and your words. Create an environment where they will feel safe, and don't punish without good reason. Better engage in conversation with them; ask, for example:

- "What is your opinion about smoking?"

- "Why is it bad for your health to smoke?"

These questions will help you begin to talk about the issue; you will exchange ideas, and there will be more of a chance that they will listen to what you have to say. Let your child draw a conclusion, and you can get an answer, for example, "I smoke because I want to feel more independent." Don't make them feel pressured into talking because you will have to. Rather, talk to your child about an uncomfortable topic in your car or when you go for a walk if you think that direct talk would make the situation even worse. In addition, if your child doesn't want to talk about smoking at the moment, that's okay; agree to talk about it in the near future.

However, if you want a good relationship with your child when they grow up, you should begin actively listening to them when they are young, even if their problems seem like no big deal to you. Your child may feel sad and not be able to express the emotions that they feel, but with active listening, you can help them. It may not be easy for you if you have had problems during the day or are doing something else. However, for your child, it is still important that you find time to talk to them because it increases the chances that they will share with you not only their desires but also their difficulties and listen to you when you want to say something.

Here is the situation: Let's say you drove to pick up your daughter from preschool. You notice her crying, and she tells you about a friend taking away her toy that she likes a lot and showing her tongue. Use a reflection and repeat what she said, not with the same words but with similar ones. You can say it in more detail or correct grammar mistakes, for instance, "So you are sad because your friend took your toy." She keeps crying and shows agreement by moving her head up and down, and she adds that her friend may break it.

You can show further that you didn't stop listening to her and say, "And you are afraid he may break it." It helps your daughter feel less upset, and you follow up with a talk that helps her understand there is nothing wrong with feeling worried. Thus, you helped her learn to name the problem and express her feelings.

Communication is even more complex when you are a narcissistic parent who has the bad habit of continuously focusing on themselves and talking a lot. Your child, if not too young, can accept it as a genuine disability, just like someone who is deaf and is not able to hear. Narcissistic parents think that they are always right and may respond to what they don't like with an irritating voice tone.

But if you want to change and become a better listener, you have to learn how to properly react to your child's difficult behavior. Negative responses, like shouting or criticizing angrily, may make it possible for your child to behave the same way someday again. Moreover, ensure that you do not criticize their behavior by referring to them as a person. For example, don't say, "I don't like being untidy," but rather, "I don't like seeing your clothes laying on the floor."

When a child is young, you must communicate with them effectively by using simple words or a dialect that they understand. Don't forget about using the right tone! Being on the same level as them helps, you have better connections and feel safer, respected, and loved. Use question words like "why," "how," and "what" to develop their ability to understand storytelling and the addition of necessary details. Set a good example for your child without the use of critical words, which will help them develop emotionally and form positive relationships. Remember, having a toddler or preschooler requires a lot of attention from you, as well as non-verbal communication like approval of something good they have done, and they need to be:

- Hugged

- Kissed

- Admired

They also need to:

- Have eye-to-eye contact with you.

- Get a high-five to show your approval for their accomplishments.

• Share facial expressions with you (e.g., a smile that gives encouragement).

When the attention given to your child is more negative than positive, it becomes a real issue, and ignoring emotional outbursts can be a better solution to decreasing the occurrence of bad behavior. However, praise your child when you see them behaving appropriately, for instance, in line at the grocery store, and say, "Thank you for your good behavior and standing next to me." However, be specific when praising; don't just say "You are good," because they need to know what behavior is good. In addition to that, it is better not to give a reward such as candy for just normal behavior because it will help only for a short period of time. It will not define the line that shouldn't be crossed and build mistrust between you. Your expectations of your child must be realistic and specific in terms of what behavior is acceptable to you.

You want to get to know your child better, so don't judge them when they express their feelings with words. Try to be empathic and listen; try to understand what they feel from their point of view, such as through angry outbursts. Help them to express in words what they experience, for instance, "I feel scared; I feel annoyed; I feel ashamed." Moreover, it is not always easy to become a better listener, and you may not clearly understand or correctly define what your child feels. Don't worry because they can fix you and say "no," and you can offer more examples to describe their feelings, such as "I feel drowsy."

Furthermore, don't judge your child's emotions and repeat what they say to you, but not with the same words; for example, if your child says, "Marco and I are not playmates anymore," and you say, "You stopped playing with him?" In this way, they can freely express their emotions without hearing judgments, and you will be astonished at how much they can tell.

To Be Understood

All your child wants is to be understood, so the ultimate goal is effective communication. Anne, who is an adult now and a mother herself, had a comparatively normal childhood with her parents because she was an obedient child, but things changed once she was transitioning. In other people's eyes, her parents wanted to be viewed as successful workers and important members of the community. However, they completely ignored their daughter's psychological wellness, were emotionally distant, and didn't agree with her wish to be able to decide for herself what she wanted.

As usual, for narcissistic parents, they were occupied with their own image and wanted to shape her into the specific image they desired. Anne's parents were unhappy when she left home because her parents had so much control over her. No wonder she wasn't successful in relationships with men, but once she met a woman, she was happy with her. Of course, her parents were disappointed when they learned about her decision, felt shame, and introduced her to a friend's son, a lawyer.

Clearly, her parents wanted her to be "normal" and socially accepted in society, which increased her anxiety. Eventually, she was taken to the hospital after taking pills and wanting to commit suicide. Anne especially felt lonely at the hospital due to her anxiety and depression, and it was even worse when her parents did not visit her there. Just because she seemed like a "threat" to her narcissistic parents, who failed to be their extensions, she was punished for not showing love and support.

How to avoid making the same mistakes as Anne's parents and how to communicate with your child more effectively without allowing negative aspects of your narcissism to interfere. Things become harder when you have a child who is in the process of transition. It is a time when they

- Want to experience something new.

- Go beyond the limit.

- Lose their temper easily and often.

Your primary responsibility as a parent is to build trust and a healthy relationship with your child. Be patient, because a teenager may not want to talk to you even about their day, though they are open to their friends through SMS. Be sure; this phase won't last forever.

Try to be understanding of their feelings rather than solving their problems. When they fail in a romantic relationship, for example, they don't want to hear you say, "I told you that boy wasn't right for you," but instead show empathy by saying, "A situation appears serious." This is how they want to be treated: as worthy of respect and trust. It helps them feel more confident and deal successfully with rising issues.

Be ready to control your emotions because, for you as an adult, it is easier than for a teenager. Yes, they can sometimes be rude and not be able to think logically because they feel upset. Before you respond, calm down and breathe deeply. If you see that both of you feel very angry, wait until you stop feeling this way and talk.

Watch for changes in your child's mood, behavior, or eating habits. When needed, ask what happened, and be a supportive parent if you notice they stop doing things that make them happy or become isolated because it can lay the foundation for resolving difficulties that may arise. Don't judge. Better, seek to get help from a therapist.

Being a good communicator is essential to parenting. Words are not always necessary; just sit with your child when they feel unhappy and ease their trouble. Be there for your child in both good and bad times. Spend some time together doing something fun that you both like, such as:

- Preparing food.

- Going for long walks.

- Going to watch a film.

Let them know that you can spend quality time together without bothering them with questions or criticism. Likewise, sit down with the whole family and eat, but agree not to use mobile phones. Have everyday conversations, for instance, about politics or sports. When your children feel comfortable talking about daily things, they will not be afraid to open up to you in hard times.

Show that you fully trust in them and that you deserve their respect. Ask your child to do something, but voluntarily, when you need help, as they will feel more confident and be able to successfully deal with difficult situations. This will help you develop the trust bond needed in any parent-child relationship.

Moreover, make your child feel appreciated and praise what they did right too, though it might look like little children need it more. In addition, you may think that your child is unconcerned about your approval, but this is not the case. It will help for both of you to be more positive and have a good relationship.

If you want to be a good parent, try to hear and understand your children from the moment they are little until they leave home and become independent adults. During their development, be reliable, supportive, encouraging, attentive, and give them space when needed. Don't be too controlling; let them make mistakes and learn from them. Respect their opinion, and they will respect yours too. Help them to form the right self-perception and be able to maintain good and emotionally deep relationships with other people in the future, including you.

5

YOU BEFORE ME

To raise a child, you need to make sacrifices, but if you're a parent with narcissistic traits, you may struggle with caring about others' needs.

Dangers of "Me First" Mentality

Being a good parent doesn't mean being perfect, and it is easier to say than to do. In 1953, Donald Winnicott, a British psychologist, gave a definition that, put simply, is when you are good enough most of the time, make mistakes at times, and outperform yourself. It is crucial when your child is having problems transitioning and requires your attention more than ever before. When it comes to dealing with separation, it becomes even more difficult.

Giving enough attention to a child, themselves, and anyone else is hard for a parent because there is a limit to their capabilities. Don't forget that you need to find time for yourself and relax. Spend time with people who make you happy to be able to help your child emotionally. For example, if they are taking an exam or someone bullies them, you must pay closer attention to them.

Worse, one of your parents is ill, or you have lost your job. It makes you feel so bad that you spend more time with yourself and leave less time for your child. When it comes to separation, your child needs all of your attention to operate properly as a person. Then you realize that there is much more time needed for everything that you are able to give, like double the time.

The research concludes that a good parent is responsive, makes their child happy, has their needs in mind, is honest, and is conscious (Rudkin, 2019). As a good parent, you are capable of hearing what your child wants to say, being attentive, and exchanging your thoughts and feelings with them. Overall, it entails putting your child's needs ahead of your own and making sacrifices for their well-being. For example, you may think that your child is unhappy about something but not respond to their contentment. Not everyone is equally sympathetic, but we react appropriately to the feelings and emotions of those we consider important in our lives.

What does it mean to prioritize your child? You may recall yourself as a child in order to empathize with them. However, memories are not always helpful because you may forget something, so you read books about raising children. You can also simply ask them how they feel at the moment, and don't be disappointed if you don't get an answer promptly.

Nevertheless, for narcissistic parents, it may be difficult to treat them as more important than themselves. If a parent is highly narcissistic, they may fail to care for their child's emotional and physical well-being. Their child lacks support, which is a form of abuse, and they

• Do not feel safe or supervised (e.g., dirty clothes and hair; increased risk of physical harm).

• Don't have a proper education (e.g., might be expelled from school because they don't have enough time for homework due to a lot of domestic tasks).

• Are emotionally neglected (e.g., other people might treat them without respect).

And their

• Health may be in poor condition (e.g., don't get proper medical treatment for infections and illnesses).

A narcissistic parent can care a little or completely abandon their child. Unfortunately, children of chronically narcissistic parents don't learn how to live without their care and don't seek ways to survive. They make an effort to hide their physical and emotional weakness, but eventually, they fail, begin to feel shame, and hate it. For example, if they feel constantly hungry, they will look for food somewhere else, such as a friend or neighbor.

Sometimes parents may feel pressure from society to properly take care of their child, and if so, they do it, but not regularly and only under certain conditions. Then they pretend that they care about their children and don't change anything about their behavior. As a consequence, such parents expect to receive more than they give because they don't feel like they have to do it. For example, they expect their child to do some kind of favor or get a lot of recognition for taking care of them.

Due to the feeling of having the right to be specially treated, narcissistic parents become too busy with their own emotional needs. They expect that these should be more important than those of their children. To them, their children are empathic listeners to their problems and strong emotions, but they never do the same in return because, in their view, they don't deserve their love, and they do it whenever they feel the need to. Usually, they think their children can read their minds and know what their parents want. However, if their children try to talk about their feelings, they may call them easily offended, upset, and tell them how they should feel.

This is because they think they can get anything without much effort, but if they can't get that attention, they feel unhappy and may threaten to abandon them, which is emotional blackmail. Parents' inability to be selfless can have a negative impact on their children, as they may be unable to meet their children's basic needs. As a consequence, they learn to stop expressing what they need because their parents don't care about it. If both parents are narcissists, their child can become manipulative to meet their needs, looking for love and warm approval from other family members and friends.

How to Be a Selfless Parent

The modern world is drowning in individualism, where everybody cares too much about themselves, but being a narcissistic parent is not a natural trait. They can acquire it over time because they did not receive adequate attention and care from their own parents when they were young. This psychological damage can come from generation to generation. Anything could have happened—maybe their own parents spoiled them or didn't teach them how to behave properly because there was no dynamic in the family.

Such a scenario is possible when they are the only child and don't have to share anything with their siblings, therefore becoming self-centered and having a little bit of empathy or none at all. Don't forget the fact that parents can have both positive and negative traits. The reasons, of course, could have been worse, such as:

- Sexual, physical, or mental abuse.

Or another, for instance:

- Irrational behaviors.

- Refusing to change.

- Family stories mixed with fantasy to feel honored.

If you are a mild narcissist and not someone with extremes in behavior who would not admit their fault and make it almost impossible to change, you can learn how to be a selfless parent and not lose your child. In your case, you may draw on the support of education, therapy, or just a friend to understand what is appropriate behavior. Admittedly, it may require a great deal of effort and dedication to become a better parent at being altruistic, generous, and understanding. Nevertheless, it is worth everything because living selfishly can make your life very hard and lead to isolation and unhappiness.

In time, you will begin to see yourself, your children, and everything around you from a different perspective. The help from other people is necessary because they may help to observe your behavior, determine if there are any deviations from norms, and help you become more kind. To learn about uncomfortable feelings and emotions you may experience and finding your true self, you can read self-help books.

The first and very important step to creating even slightly better relationships with your own children, which will help you become less preoccupied with yourself and more self-aware, is to learn to listen. First, you will have to stop talking about yourself when you feel lacking in importance and not receiving proper attention and learn that listening to others is not a waste of your time. Stop thinking that your opinion or attitude is the most accurate and start listening to what they want to say. Be prepared to

- Ask questions.

Engage physically in what they want to say to you

- Reply to questions in an appropriate manner.

- Nod with your head.

Allow your child to speak without any preconceived notions or stories you may wish to share. Be aware of the present moment you spend together, get to know them, and connect with them emotionally. This will be a small step toward becoming a compassionate parent. What else can you do? Try to see things the way your child sees them. Imagine the pain that they are suffering and the problems that they are dealing with.

Maybe you felt the same way before. What feelings have you experienced? For example, you may have lost self-respect or felt unhappy. Understand that the human in front of you can feel, react, and have the same problems as you. Remember and share how you felt during the worst and best times of your life.

Step by step, try to become a more empathetic and compassionate parent, and genuinely care about your child as much as you do about yourself. Find out what they desire and need. If you do it, you will make a big change. It is very true that we all have some narcissistic traits necessary for survival, and healthy ones mean that you have a balance between your own and your child's needs without giving or taking too much or too little. It will help you be more sensitive to others' feelings.

Find time in the morning, during the day, or in the afternoon, for example, to spend with your child that is not only about complimenting or giving hugs. It's about finding a place in your life, so be attentive to their concerns when they need it, or just give them some company. In this way, you will not only develop a close relationship with your child, but also share the deep beliefs that you left behind.

A child can bring many positives to the relationship. Particularly when you spend time together, create memories, and open up to each other without wanting to change anything in the past or make an impact on the future. As you recall those memories, they may help you overcome the challenges coming in the future. Through communication with your child, you can learn that controlling everything and everyone is not possible except for yourself. Learning this lesson can help you avoid wasting energy on conflicts and enjoy the moment with the ones you love and care about.

Still, for a narcissistic parent, it is necessary to understand that children need to get emotional and physical support from their parents. Without them, they feel vulnerable and put themselves in danger. Especially at a young age, they can't defend themselves because they have a small amount of knowledge about the world. Worse still, if parents neglect a teenager, they might try drugs or injure themselves because they feel lonely and depressed. As adults, they may also only see threats around them, and it can be hard to separate from their parents and begin an independent life. Also, they may seek status and prove that they are better than anyone and successful, and they may become materialistic.

A good parent gives their child enough attention and prioritizes their needs. It is extremely difficult for highly narcissistic parents who are concerned only with themselves and abandon their children, both physically and emotionally. Such children become very vulnerable and don't have knowledge of how to survive. However, it is possible to become a selfless parent with a lot of work, like an active listener without interruption and without imposing their view.

They will have to learn to be empathic and attentive to their child's concerns, and they can learn positive things from their relationship with them. Therefore, understanding that the well-being and future of a child depend on their parents, who provide necessary support and protection, is crucial.

6

DEFUSING THE BOMB

It is hard to keep your cool in stressful situations when raising a child with difficult behavior traits, but luckily, there are strategies to do so.

The Narcissistic Rage

In 1972, American psychoanalyst Heinz Kohut offered the term "narcissistic rage." In simple terms, it is when someone with NPD experiences a sudden attack of anger or quietness that they can't control and don't care about the consequences for other people. A person with NPD reacts with rage, which is the most common reaction, including various repetitive actions and emotions. For example, a lack of ability to control anger, becoming angry because something is not right according to your beliefs, and an invisible bitterness because you were forced to do something you don't want to do.

It's normal for us to want to be admired and get attention from other people, but that's not the case for people with NDP. When they don't get the attention they think they deserve, they may react with intense anger. Therefore, they can either start screaming and shouting loudly or be completely silent and avoid the threat to their perception of themselves. In the sense that they can act cool and avoid communication with other people. This is because they want to hurt someone and feel as if they are not there, but the "targets" should completely ignore this kind of behavior. They should neither accept it nor say, "I am sorry," because it's not their fault.

Moreover, those outbursts of rage and violent behavior stem from a desire to defend themselves. It does not always mean that you suffer from narcissistic rage when you get angry, because anyone can experience that. For example, you might get angry because:

- Someone put their car in your parking space.

- Your boss promised but didn't increase your salary.

- Your child got a negative result from homework.

Narcissistic rage is just a part of NPD, and there can be other disorders similar to this trait, such as persecutory delusions or manic depression. The causes of this disorder may be genetics, the way they were treated by their parents, and the experiences they had. There are three reasons why episodes of narcissistic rage occur:

- **Damage to self-confidence and sense of self-worth** (people with NPD believe they are better than everyone else is, but their self-confidence is fragile, and when they are hurt, they defend themselves verbally and physically).

- **Impaired confidence** (false identities and lies "help" people with NPD become more confident, but when someone reveals their qualities of being weak and can't deal with the situation, they attack someone verbally or physically).

- **Being doubtful about self-perception** (when someone reveals that people with NDP are not so talented or who they claim to be, they act aggressively).

Getting angry is a natural component of our lives, but it can be very damaging at home in front of children when not managed. It is especially unhealthy when parents have arguments in front of their children. A parent with narcissistic rage becomes enraged; they wish to emotionally destroy a family member. It may feel like, in this state, they want to kill that person. In order to survive this mode, a victim needs to show that they are afraid and accept responsibility for the blame.

One of the survivors of parental outbursts is Perry, whose father, who was very distrustful and expressed contempt, constantly shouted at his mother during childhood. It was not difficult at all for him to find reasons to criticize or hate Perry's mother. The sad truth is that she patiently suffered those outbursts of anger and the banging of fists on the table from her husband until the moment he was done with them. The situation could have been worse if the mother or Perry had replied in a rude way or left the room. The freezing technique helped Perry reduce the harm.

The type of anger in this situation is indirect because the real victim was Perry's mother, who was still affected by the negative emotions that his father expressed. Words were not the most important thing a father said to his wife because children, when they are little, can't distinguish between thoughts and emotions. It is how those words, how he spoke and behaved, and his tone of voice affected Perry. He became empathic when his mother was subjected to his father's rage and learned how not to communicate with a family member.

Narcissistic rage can cause emotional pain and physical and emotional harm, especially to family members who are unfairly punished. Typically, parents act this way because they

- Are exhausted after a long day at work.

- Get less sleep than needed.

- Have problems with money.

- Don't have time for themselves.

It's natural to feel angry when you are stressed, but not to turn it into verbal and psychological aggression against your family members. That is why parents who suffer from NPD should seek help from psychiatrists or psychologists:

- To understand the reasons for their behavior.

- What choices they can make.

- And what the effects of such behaviors are.

A specialist may help them to develop new coping mechanisms to deal with stressful events and the ability to maintain healthy relationships. Luckily, nowadays there are many options on how to manage narcissistic rage, such as anger management therapy classes, online courses, or neurotherapy. Therapy for family and marriage is extremely helpful because you will learn how not to become angry in front of your child and not to leave long-term effects. It will also aid in understanding the difference between the psychology of adults and children and how to stay connected.

A parent with NPD will learn about their true selves and how to control themselves through therapy. They will also learn not to want to appear better and manipulate others. However, the most important step at the beginning of healing is to admit that a change in behavior is necessary to change the situation, move forward, and have healthy relationships.

Losing Your Control

The diagnosis of narcissistic rage is not the only reason or case why parents can't control their own feelings and actions. Parenting itself may result in a full bouquet of emotions, from excitement to loss of hope. For example, if a child is less than one year old, they don't understand what behavior is appropriate. And, by all means, their parents should not hit or shake them, though there are parents who think that it's the right way to teach them discipline, which is absolutely not. This causes irreversible mental and physical damage (for example, to the neck, which holds a large head and causes muscle damage) and can result in death, disability, or serious injury. When children are just babies, all they need from their parents is love and care.

Even if they love and are proud of their children, some circumstances may cause them to become enraged if they raise them. Every parent should understand that children observe how their parents act and learn to imitate them. If they see their parents engaging in abusive behavior, they will eventually act like that, and it will become difficult for them to control their emotions.

Here is a typical real-life scenario: Let's say you had a really busy day at work, and after it is over, you feel anxious. You pick up your child from school and argue angrily with each other. It causes annoyance and emotional strain. To make matters worse, when you come back home, your child doesn't put their things, like a box for lunch or their school bag, in the right places.

It would be better for you as a parent to teach your child what they did wrong and what they have to do next time to avoid unnecessary disputes. Do it without strong emotions and emphasize what you want to say verbally and physically. Otherwise, a child may be disrespectful to you and refuse to listen to you when you tell them to do something. You may become enraged and respond by doing the same, but later apologizing. Take this situation or one similar to it as a message that tells you to spend more time with your child to create a sense of closeness. Every parent, including you, should have in mind that their child is in the process of development and when they do, they will react appropriately and feel less stress.

Maybe the difficult behavior of a child means that there are no dynamics in a family. If anger constantly arises in a parent when a child misbehaves, there is probably a lot of hard discipline within a family, which they should avoid most of the time. What parents want is proper behavior, but first, they have to learn how to communicate with their significant other. The most common reason for anger is parenting stress and irritation that a child feels too.

If a child sees their parents constantly angry or aggressive, it can have a very negative impact on them, and they can blame themselves for that. A child experiences emotional strain, which can have an impact on their development and be the reason for mental health disorders or health problems, such as inflammation or headaches in adulthood. The feeling of not being good enough can develop gradually if their parents are shouting at them too. They show their anger to a parent in the same way they did it to them, and it causes negative behavior where no one takes responsibility for their actions.

Children can't still think rationally, and they won't until their brains are fully developed at 25 years old, so such a negative response is natural to them. Therefore, a child may have sleeping problems, become ill, and be very quiet. However, if parents' anger turns into physical abuse, for example, if they slap their child, they can act aggressively or not trust themselves and not be successful in the future, even becoming antisocial. Moreover, the study conducted in 2017—which surveyed 350 adults about 50 years old living on the street—showed that they were very psychologically and physically abused when growing up (*How Parental Anger Can Affect Children*, 2022). As a result, it is necessary to foster a healthy relationship between a child and their parents because it demonstrates the right path in life.

Managing Your Anger

It is important to remain calm with your child during situations that cause you stress, and there are many tips and strategies on how to do it. Anger is only good when it is a source of energy to finish something or defend your opinion. However, getting angry with your child quite often and being hard to control is very harmful to them. No matter how difficult at times they can be to handle, they need to grow up feeling secure and safe, free of conflicts and shouting. React when your body sends you a message of growing anger inside you that involves physical symptoms, which will help prevent your outbursts of anger:

- increased pulse rate

- queasy feeling in your stomach

- skin color changes to red

- anxiety

- rapid breathing

- tight muscles

- emitting sweat

When you are angry, it is normal to think negatively, which can degrade a situation; therefore, it is important to protect yourself against negative thinking. Foremost, try to forget problems related to work and not bring them home so as not to make a negative impact on communication with your child. It would be great if you agreed to get angry, apologize to your child, and talk about what happened and how you didn't mean it. In this way, you would show a good example of how to manage anger and irritability, and it is not good to act like this.

You may believe, for example, that your child is disobedient; you may wonder why they are acting this way or whether you would be so angry if they weren't. If you catch yourself thinking like that, you need to do something about it and find ways to stop feeling this way until you can't control yourself and react violently emotionally. You want to enjoy your parenting, so it would be good if you talked with other parents about their experiences and feelings that can be quite similar to yours. You are not the only one with such an attitude and values toward raising a child, so join a parent group. It's not only your problem. An exchange of opinions with other parents on raising difficult children can also be helpful because you can share problems and tips on how to solve them in the future.

First, you can start working with yourself and noticing when you become angry at others and even at yourself. Then you can try to clarify all the triggers and get rid of them.

Though you can't leave your child alone, you can relax very soon if you take these steps:

- Breathe slowly, breathing out and in for several minutes.

- Count up to 10 at a slow speed.

- Put on headphones that reduce background noise, such as your child's screams, and breathe deeply several times.

Before you take a few minutes to yourself, leave your child in the care of responsible adults:

- Look through a magazine or read a book.

- Go outside and inhale some air.

It's good if you can find more time to spend with yourself:

- Clean yourself in the shower or bath.

- Do yoga, meditate, or exercise regularly.

- Take care of your garden.

- Go to the hairdressing saloon.

- Talk with your friend about your feelings.

A good way to begin handling a situation is to tell your child that you feel angry at the moment and need to relax. Ideally, find some place where you can be alone with yourself. Eventually, you will notice that you begin to feel less upset, with a slower pulse rate and relaxed muscles and shoulders. When you finally feel calm, think carefully about the situation and what you experienced, as this may help you to manage similar ones in the future, and ask yourself questions, for example, "What made me feel so angry?" "Was it worth it to react this way?" or "How do I want to resolve this situation?" Just remember that from time to time, it is normal to face negative emotions, and parenting is not an easy task that involves a lot of responsibilities.

Keeping your cool and not exploding from anger outbursts is the best way to get out of uncomfortable and difficult situations. Anything can make a parent angry, without necessarily having narcissistic rage traits, but if they do, the situation is much more difficult. Anger itself is very harmful, not only to the parent but also to the child, and can have long-term physical and psychological damage when a child becomes an adult. Parenting is never easy because parents have problems and many responsibilities themselves. Using rational thinking to solve problems with difficult children while avoiding verbal and physical abuse is something various tips and strategies can help develop.

7

FAIR SHARE
OF THE BLAME

There is always more than one person to blame; both parents and children should take accountability for their actions, but a parent must have enough information on how to be fair in the process.

It's On Me

Admit that it's not so easy to recognize the consequences of the choices you made, the actions you took, and the way you behaved in certain situations. That's how Tedd Harmand, a management consultant, defines personal accountability. It means that you don't just blame others, which would be the easiest way to get out of the situation you're in, but you try to repair it as much as you can. You are fully aware that dealing with it may have both positive and negative consequences.

The meaning of another term, "responsibility," is similar to "accountability" but has some different characteristics. When you take responsibility, it means that you have to comply with the rules, but when you accept accountability for something, you agree with the outcomes. As a parent, you, like many other parents, may struggle with admitting mistakes in raising a child and treating them unfairly, as well as accepting responsibility for all of this. A story of a mother and her son demonstrates how true this is.

When a boy was in sixth grade, it was easy for him to make excuses for not doing his homework, which turned out to be his mother's problem. The teacher accused her of being irresponsible and not taking care that her son would do his homework. A boy became manipulative and acted as a victim until the end of the eighth grade, when his mother finally admitted that it was all her fault. For two years, it was difficult for a mother to accept the fact that she was not a good parent. That is why she denied the teacher's accusations and became her own worst enemy.

She talked with her son in an unpleasant tone and absorbed all the negativity. He even told the teacher that his mother doesn't like her and becomes angry when she calls her. It really helped the way a mother responded to the teacher's worries about her son. It's good that she didn't take everything personally because the teacher wants to help determine the reasons why her son isn't doing his homework. The reason was that his mother didn't teach him to accept responsibility and accountability for what he does. The study conducted in 2007 shows that parents should encourage their children to take responsibility for what they do, which helps them to interact more positively (Mind Tools Content Team, n.d.-a).

However, if you're a narcissistic parent yourself, you want to avoid responsibility so that you don't admit to being wrong. If you do, it should be for things that have no value other than to help you get attention. You may think other people may want to control you this way, so you try to escape it. The aim of a narcissist is to avoid blame at all costs, so you may:

• Intimidate and blame others when you don't want to be accountable for your actions, and you will see it as their aim to make you not look great.

• Deny any responsibility, and you will find reasons why you don't have to do something and say that you were forced to be accountable, which will make another person doubt what they said.

• Accuse and project someone else instead of yourself who is very responsible and admires you, and you successfully run away from accusations.

• Retreat after another person tells you that you are irresponsible because not giving them attention and love and saying that they aren't grateful for help, so the victim takes the responsibility and adores you even more.

If you struggle with narcissism, you should take responsibility for becoming more responsible and trustworthy. Why is it important? Being a narcissist is bad for you because you constantly deny everything: reality, events that happened, your actions, the good deeds of other people, and the negative results of your bad behavior. If you do it constantly, you will finally believe it more than reality. It's very hard for you to solve problems because you deny what's real, and solutions to them are not usual.

If you take the right actions, people will trust and respect you more, and it will be easier for you to communicate, which is especially important in your workplace, not only within your family. You will also save time because your actions will show your true attitude, and if problems arise, you will be able to solve them easily and prevent bad consequences. Luckily, responsibility is not a trait you must genetically inherit and that you lack due to your behavioral impairment and incompetence, and there are strategies to learn it.

Always be sincere with yourself and with others, and if you make mistakes or take wrong actions, recognize them and apologize for them. It's normal for problems to arise, and you can solve them by trusting your intuition or talking to somebody to help you. But never put the blame on someone else for something you did wrong; only think about yourself in that situation. Better express regret for making mistakes and correct them. Everyone who is in that situation with you will pay attention to the object, but not to the problem itself. Deal with a problem on time; don't delay solving it; if you do, people won't trust you.

It may be that you lack information to solve a problem; look for it and solve it. Remember that only you are responsible for your actions and choices. Maybe there are situations where you should have taken responsibility but didn't. Think about them. You can learn from them. Think about the changes that you can make about yourself. What differences can you make?

Accountability and Consequences

You, who have difficulties with narcissism, need to learn how you can teach your child to be honestly accountable and responsible, which is one of the most important lessons in life. It will help them learn to control their thoughts and emotions and behave properly. As usual, children cause challenges to their parents and do something beyond their limits, and parents try to make them act normally but without success.

They don't listen to their parents and pay no attention to warnings about being punished for bad behavior. It's necessary to establish a clear plan for what parents should do when their children break the rules, as well as the consequences. They should take it seriously. Be patient, because gaining your child's trust and understanding takes time, and ensuring that you do what you say is essential. It's possible that your child will change their behavior and begin to listen to you. Show positive attention to your child, which is important for discipline, and do it for approximately 15 minutes every day. For example:

- Talk.

- Bake something together.

- Read a story.

- Look through the photo album and share your memories.

Give that time only to them and avoid using your phone, though you might think that they don't notice that. Clarify the consequences; don't say, "You can't go anywhere until I let you," because that won't sound serious or clear enough. 24 hours should be enough time for the consequences to be effective. Say to your child, "You won't get this toy back until the same hour tomorrow."

Sometimes you can shorten the time of punishment, for example, if they keep everything in order in their room and demonstrate positive behavior. Explain to them what they need to do to get something back that someone took from them. It will be clear how they should behave, and you will avoid disputes. With the use of this approach, you place emphasis on the child's behavior and consequences.

Clearly state what you expect from them and set restrictions. For example, you don't let your children use abusive language and say, "It's forbidden in this house to use abusive names referring to other people. I had never made you angry, and no one had ever called you that. If you do it, I'll take your toys from you." If children start paying attention to something else, say, "You put the blame on your brother, though you started first." Your children use abusive language as a defense because they feel insecure.

Make it clear that it's not acceptable to put the blame on someone. Everyone is equal in the house and must take responsibility and accountability for their actions and follow the rules and do what is expected of them, which should be clear. They also should be able to take responsibility for their response to difficult situations. You can put those rules on the refrigerator as a reminder.

A child should know that the family can't change the rules if someone doesn't like them. For example, they can't play with their computer until they can speak without using abusive names for two hours. Knowing about consequences and motivation may help a child change their behavior as well as make for a better parent-child relationship.

Narcissistic parents themselves may struggle with accountability, which helps them grow, learn from mistakes, and live according to their beliefs and attitudes. The majority of us learned when we were little what things were good and bad, but when you are a narcissistic parent, you may find it hard to accept your mistakes and correct them, understand your feelings, and say sorry. It might be difficult for you to determine the level of accountability your child should take in a given situation because you yourself

- Always find excuses for your actions and find someone else to put the blame on.

- May feel better than others.

- Think that you are more important than others.

- Find it hard to be emphatic and to show it.

You should understand that if there is a lack of accountability in the family, a child, when grown up, might face difficulties with self-esteem. They will not be able to feel safe or trust other people, and they will see danger everywhere. There are moments in everyone's life when we do something wrong and admit that, and it's normal to make mistakes. If you want to be an emotionally healthy parent, you should work on accountability and teach your child. If not, it might be difficult for you to administer fairly disciplinary measures for bad behavior. However, there are recommendations and strategies that can help you deal with those issues and become a better parent.

Don't let your child find reasons to do something that they shouldn't. Instead, teach them to acknowledge that they made a mistake and to think about ways they can prevent it in the future, but you as a narcissistic parent must be able to be accountable first, for example, at your work. For example, you needed to safely deliver light bulbs but many of them were broken and you are accountable and need to take responsibility for the breakage. You need to understand that it's important and you will in time though you might not like it because, if not, you will lose your job.

Also, you may need to explain to your boss what you will do next time to avoid such a situation, and you will probably need to work longer to fix the problem. This kind of situation teaches you responsibility and meets the expectations of others, and if you learn it, you will be able to teach it to your children too. Your child should learn only to leave a class to calm down if they feel very unhappy and not express extreme anger toward classmates. For example, if they become calm, they won't be throwing things, shouting, or closing doors violently. Yes, it may sound hard to do, but it will help them become responsible and successful adults.

You and your child should both learn things you don't want to do but must do in order to be healthy and function normally as adults in the future. For instance, you need to talk with a teacher on the phone. An adequate amount of time, like one day, is necessary to think clearly about the situation and what you are going to say. It will help you to react in a suitable manner, and though your instinct is to protect your child from harm, you have to respect the opinion of your teacher too. In this way, you will demonstrate to your child the importance of showing respect to others in order to be a successful member of society. They will use this skill in their future as students and workers, and it will help them create healthy relationships with other people.

Parents need to teach their children to be accountable and responsible for their actions, but in order to do this; they need to be like that. It's never too late; and both can learn it through practice. It's important for parents to raise awareness of the rules and consequences at home for children to learn how to behave, and they will be able to do so outside of their home.

8

IN THE CONTROL SEAT

It's no good if parents take full control of their child's life, and it can do a lot of damage to their future. Parents, and especially those with narcissistic traits, should be aware of that mistake.

Beware of the Iron Grip

Your duty is to be fully present while raising your child from the day they are born until they become adults and to make sure that they are safe and healthy, keeping in mind their needs. What does it look like? With you as a good parent, they are emotionally connected and want to spend time together.

You emphasize what you expect from them and set expectations for how things should be. It's all about doing things every day, learning how to communicate with each other in a proper manner, and expressing feelings such as sadness, annoyance, and displeasure. You have to use this model of child rearing throughout your child's development.

Your responsibility is to provide good guidance; therefore, you decide what activities your child takes part in. For example, your child needs to clean their room even though they don't want to do it. Your job is not to demand it and yell at it, but to clean it willingly. Saying they won't go anywhere until they do doesn't work. Consider your child's personality: will he simply refuse it, or can you encourage them with something amusing, such as music? Moreover, just simply say that if they clean their room, maybe they will find something they lost, like another shoe from the pair, and a weekend is a good time to do it. It may work; just try it!

Nevertheless, if you deal with narcissism, you have difficulties not controlling too much, which usually ends in the overcontrol of your child. You do so because you see danger everywhere and catastrophize everything. In addition, you only see good and bad people and want to protect your child from "strangers." Then you go a step further and believe that your child is either with you or against you. Being the guardian of your child is an honor for you, but you expect them to be completely loyal and to follow your instructions. Thus, you ascertain the limits of your child's socialization with other people, and if they want to take some kind of risk, you see it as a breach of trust.

You use some tactics to maintain control over your child's life. Manipulations come in many forms: you make them feel guilty, don't show affection, and threaten not to give them money to meet their needs. For example, your child, who is approximately six years old, had an unpleasant situation at school and did something they were forbidden to do. After all, they feel bad and are afraid that if you found out the truth, you wouldn't love them as much as you do or would love another sibling more who is unproblematic. They feel pain inside because they need to control that feeling and situation and want to look perfect to you as you imagine them. Your child feels bad because they feel the need to control themselves like you do; if not, their inner defense system is activated.

You also use a psychological form of manipulation that makes your child doubt themselves. Because you deny the words you said, repeat their words but in a different manner, and act as if you "forgot" that you were angry or aggressive at that moment. Moreover, you can become aggressive, not be able to control your emotions, start shouting, and start crying. This causes very traumatizing psychological damage to your child, and they can be afraid of their own and other people's anger.

If you were a child who always followed the rules, you might be upset if your child does the opposite. It makes you very angry when they don't do what you say and, at the same time, are not in control of your child. This makes you even angrier and causes you to shout even louder, which you may believe will make them fear you and listen to you. However, a child started crying, including yourself. You didn't like the way you felt, and you didn't mean it. Everything is because of childhood trauma because you were a very good child and listened to your parents, even though you didn't agree with what they did and said but didn't want to disappoint them.

A child may also have to suffer constant criticism from you. For example, if they want to be closer to you but you're afraid of becoming too vulnerable and rejecting them with a harsh remark, they don't trust you even though they thought they could. Additionally, you want your child to meet your needs, so you shape their personality as you want, and they think that they are emotionally dependent on you because they are weak and need your attention. For instance, let's say you have an 11-year-old daughter, and every time you have a conflict, you talk about it afterward. They feel happy to share that time alone with you even though they know it's not good to behave badly.

That becomes the only way to connect with you, but they would like to share something positive with you. It makes them feel unsure of themselves, and they can't differentiate the reason from the consequences. If you were in a similar situation, you may catch yourself after reading this question: "Where did I make a mistake?" or "How did it happen?" If you do, you are not necessarily that bad a parent, even though you make mistakes; these are just descriptions of tendencies, and there is no such thing as a perfect parent.

Finding Balance

Occasionally, parents think and feel that their children are uncontrollable, but it doesn't last too long. However, other parents have to deal with it constantly. Their children don't listen to them, don't follow the rules, and don't care about the consequences of what they do. If you find yourself in this situation, you must take control of the situation without becoming overly dominant.

Don't use the word "control" when you speak about your child; better use "cope." Because you cannot control everything that exists. You need to cope with the situation in the best possible way, which may not always work, but that's how it is. Consider it a problem-solving method for them. Make a simple thing: take a piece of paper and draw two boxes. On one side, make a list of what you want to accomplish, and on the other, make a list of what you can do to put the first list into action.

Think about the topic, which may be "How to resolve my child's anger?" What you may want are: still evenings, to spend time with family happily, and to be able to comment on my child's homework without disagreement. All you want is for your child to be happy. The first box is not the most important one, which you can read many times, but nothing will change because the second one is what you can do. For example:

- "I will ask about their feelings."

- "I will remain level-headed."

- "I will let them show their thoughts and feelings."

Everything begins with the pronoun "I," which means that you have to start with yourself. It may be difficult, and maybe not everything will be possible to change, but the most important thing is to be on the right path, which is this step. But be careful not to force your child to behave in a way that will make you happy. All parents have certain expectations about their children in terms of who they are and will become, and you might have thought that it would be very easy with them, but all children are different, and some are more difficult than others. You need to understand their state of mind and what you need to do to make them happy. Most likely, you and your child don't understand each other's needs.

What your child says is not necessarily incorrect, and what they need is unreasonable. Listen to what they say, turn what they say into an understandable form, and react differently than you usually do. Never try to fix your child. Just know when a child needs your assistance; don't try to stop them from making mistakes; let them make them and learn from them.

However, you can still create rules and structures. You may find it hard to believe, but children aren't against setting rules and restrictions; they like them. They feel safe when their parents are effective leaders, able to decide about the rules and make them active. If you want your child to listen to you, the rules must be clear, and you can write them down together with the whole family. For instance, "Ask before you take something from another person." Involve the whole family into the routine, which will make the child's day organized. Then a child knows when it's time to

- Do their homework.

- Engage in household duties appropriate to their age.

- Have a meal.

- Take part in family activities.

- have playtime.

A way of parenting is no good if you try by psychological means to make them feel guilty about something they have done, show love if they only act good, make them feel shame, and say you decide everything in this house because it's yours. It will have a lot of negative consequences. They will lack confidence and suffer from mental disorders. They will also have worse results at school, have communication problems, be angry and irritable, and not be able to manage their emotions.

Think about yourself. Do you like being controlled? When you do something to please someone, such as at work or in your relationships with others. You feel less motivation and satisfaction and do not enjoy that activity or company. When you are a parent, it is even trickier because you need to find the right balance. You have to treat them as other people that you can't control, but at the same time, you can have an influence on them.

It's not about your intentions but about your child's experiences and their awareness of your control and their autonomy. Usually, parents use two types of control, such as psychological and behavioral, which have an effect on their children's motivation, which can be external or internal, and their sense of autonomy. Psychological control means a parent's effort to control their feelings, ambitions, and sense of self. In a sense, if a parent doesn't respond to their child's emotions and feelings, they damage the child's autonomy and cause problems with behavior, making them feel anxious and depressed.

Internal control, as a part of psychological control, is when you motivate your child to behave in a way that makes them feel confident about themselves, more important than others, and keeps them away from feelings of guilt and shame. If parents control them internally, they may not show affection to their child or feel angry, and thus a child will feel upset because of the lack of a satisfying connection with their parents. But when it comes to behavioral control, it is more difficult. When they control it in a healthy manner, it means structure; if not, it means pressure.

If it is healthy control, parents take care, for instance, that their child will go to school every day and have healthy eating habits that help their child develop and grow up. If parents use autonomy-supportive practices to control their child's behavior, they

- Set restrictions.

- Understand their child's emotions.

- Let the child choose what they want.

- Set clear boundaries.

- Describe the consequences if they deviate from the limits (e.g., if a child ruins the wall with paint, they need to clean it).

However, if there are no limits and a clear definition of what behavior is appropriate, parenting will not be effective and cause danger to their child's mental health and well-being. You pay attention to their needs, which they demonstrate verbally and behaviorally, and you provide what they need at that moment. Although it doesn't mean letting children take control of the house and do damage—for example, you don't let them destroy their toys or furniture—limits help your children learn responsibility, and the most important thing is how you set and enforce them.

Some parents use pressure through punishment and rewards to get their children to act in an appropriate way. It is external control, which is a subdivision of behavioral control, and has negative effects because external pressure motivates a child to behave badly accordingly. Later in life, a child can become dependent on drugs, commit crimes, and behave badly. But it doesn't mean that a child doesn't need to be motivated and warned about the consequences of their behavior.

Don't use a reward to control their bad behavior, but instead do it for a positive one. Avoid using the words "if" and "then," and instead say something like, "As soon as you finish your household tasks, we'll get together to slide downhill." As a form of reward, take your child to the shop and let them choose the goods they want. It may help motivate your child to continue to behave well.

The right balance in parenting is necessary, with less control and more autonomy, while keeping the balance. Because in this way, they will develop their self-esteem and have the right set of beliefs that will guide them throughout their lives. The intention of a parent is to teach a child to understand why it is necessary to behave in an appropriate way, not to do it because they feel the need to please us or to avoid punishment from us.

9

UNDER THE MICROSCOPE

Parents with narcissistic traits criticize more than anyone else, but there are effective strategies to combat this harmful behavior.

Perfect Is the Enemy of Good

Frequently, narcissistic parents think of themselves as leaders. They never use a conversational style with simple vocabulary and talk as if they are more intelligent than their child, though in reality, it may be the opposite. A narcissistic parent does this because they want to show their authority and make their child feel inferior, and they do so not only with their words but also physically: they glance downward at their child. Despite a child's knowledge, they never get the chance themselves to defend against the bully, and a parent always succeeds.

It can be any kind of successful achievement by a child, but a parent with narcissistic traits may say that they did it before them and were more successful and efficient. They magnify their achievements and make those of their children less important. Therefore, a child feels like they will never reach the level of their parent's level, which reinforces the authority of a parent.

A child wants, in a desperate manner, to be like their parent, who, in their opinion, has exceptional abilities. They are never satisfied with their own accomplishments and constantly judge themselves. It happens as if they start hearing their parent's inner voice, which criticizes them for not being good enough. This has a very harmful effect on children because their parents with narcissistic traits are overly critical and believe that they have to be perfect. For example, even though an A is a satisfactory result on a task, they criticize themselves because they did not receive an A+. A child becomes so anxious that they don't try to achieve what they desire, and this prevents their development.

Normally, a child wants to be close to their parents, who love them unconditionally and approve of the way they are, which is biologically important for survival. However, when their parents have narcissistic traits, it becomes impossible because they criticize and humiliate their child, making it difficult to maintain a relationship, and their love comes with conditions. They usually:

- Roll their eyes to express disapproval.

- Speak sarcastically.

- Show an unfriendly attitude.

Life with overly critical parents can lead a child to develop many emotional issues, which are not always obvious, that will degrade the quality of their lives. They will lack confidence because their parents always caused them to feel shame. Their parents raised very high expectations that they weren't able to fulfill because, in their eyes, they were just average, which is not satisfying to them. Due to the fact that it is nearly impossible to meet the needs of narcissistic parents, their children are not able to balance their emotions later in life.

A child will also develop an inferiority complex from feeling lower since their parents always compared them to other children who, according to them, were better. They were not allowed to show anger, which would have made them feel as if they had done something inappropriate, and they always had to act in a good manner. As a child grows up, if they dare, getting angry helps them escape from relationships in which they feel misunderstood and free themselves from the suppression of that feeling, which is not healthy.

Besides, if children suffer from depression when they grow up, it is all because their parents didn't sufficiently care for and protect them, and they felt that they weren't good enough. This makes it hard to create and keep relationships with themselves and anyone else. Not to mention how hard it is to love themselves. Additionally, it's possible to see anxiety and depression symptoms in children, but as they grow, they become more severe.

Moreover, children are not able to express themselves verbally because their parents didn't let them do it as they grew up. As a result, they develop speech anxiety because they do not feel confident enough to express their own opinions and are afraid to disagree with those of others. Their sense of self is also weak, which is crucial to living life normally. They always compare themselves to other people and don't feel confident about their skills. Therefore, they don't feel safe and can't control themselves. A child ends up not knowing their identity or what they want in life.

Furthermore, they may be too sensitive to everything that occurs in their lives. This is because as children, they had to react to their parents' changing moods. As they grew up, they became hypersensitive to other people's feelings and emotions. It can become hard to maintain relationships because they are overly sensitive to the smallest problems. They can't control their emotions, and others treat them unfairly to benefit from them.

Do you recognize yourself as having the narcissistic traits mentioned above, or most of them? It's time to make a change and get to know your problems that came from childhood and made bad things happen. It will be a challenge to have a normal and healthy life since a narcissistic parent raised you and instilled their beliefs. But letting go of past experience and all the things related to it can make a change!

Only Human

If you find yourself being overly critical of your child's every action, like not sitting straight on the chair or leaving shoes lying around, there are tips and strategies that can help you. The focus is on the child's safety and creating an environment where they can flourish. You can assist them, but you cannot control everything they do. Don't criticize too much because it will have negative consequences and your child will not be happy or grow up as a healthy human being. Express appropriate admiration and approval for who they are.

Criticizing everything your child does will make them focus their attention on your reaction to what they have done. You can only correct them when you really know it will persuade them to behave better in the future and you want to help them for their own good. A correction would be telling your toddler that they can't borrow toys from other children without asking. But if you took that toy from their hands and told them that they were bad, that would be criticism, which does not help them learn the lesson.

When you criticize them regularly for everything, they will not learn about their emotions at that moment, for example, feeling sad or ashamed, which are related to the unpleasant consequences of their actions. You will absorb those negative emotions from them, and they will eventually learn how others treat them poorly but not how to improve their bad behavior. Moreover, they will not develop the ability to take personal accountability and will feel like victims.

The findings of a study of 87 participants at Binghamton University in New York show that children may have difficulty identifying facial emotions if their parents are very critical of them because they want to hold off that criticism. It might be due to emotional distance from a parent when a child learns to pay attention to one thing and ignore others. However, it may be possible that a child will not be capable of recognizing not only negative emotions but also all of them, even positive ones (Campbell, 2018).

A narcissistic parent must learn not to constantly disapprove of their child's choices or behavior in order for them not to engage in socially unacceptable behavior as adults due to the desire to defend themselves. Therefore, having normal expectations of your child will not make them want to be overly competitive, which can be damaging. At times, wanting to be better than others is good, but not when it's too much. Children will only feel respect for themselves if they achieve something big; if not, they will take it very seriously.

The desire for perfection from a parent about how a child should perform at school, communicate with other people, and look in the public eye causes harm. They usually get the opposite effect because a child doesn't behave the way they want, as it should in their "ideal world." A narcissistic parent also usually thinks negatively and has a tendency to want to change something, especially their child, because they are not satisfied with how they behave and think that they do it purposefully. Instead, teach a child to communicate and express themselves properly. This will help you better understand each other and see more positivity in your relationship.

Discipline your child without shaming because it is harmful and can make them feel worthless. Let your child make mistakes if you want your child to change their behavior on their own. Your job is to help them become stronger and persuade them to try to complete a task where they made a mistake; accordingly, don't criticize them and you will gain their trust. Challenges and difficulties help them develop.

To grow up as a normal human being, a child needs supportive parents to become a happy and psychologically healthy person whose emotional, physical, social, and spiritual well-being are fulfilled. The crucial period from one to five years of their lives is when they learn how to appropriately behave, express empathy, set healthy boundaries, and develop social skills that are necessary throughout their lives. What you say and how you react to your child's difficult behavior has a huge impact on them, even when they are just infants. With those words, you should show that you

- Treat them equally.

- Understand their feelings.

- Are empathic.

Throughout the toddler stage, help your child build their character and show them affection, love, and positive emotions. Don't try to change your child's behavior and "shape" a perfect child because you want to feed your ego and be a perfect parent. If you have a child displaying difficult behavior, you can try positive parenting practices, the positive discipline method, learn more about the growth and development process of a child, and study neuropsychology to learn about the child's behavior and cognition. All of this can give you more knowledge and help you act in the right way when raising a child.

Over time, you will learn to manage negative judgments about your child, even though it's not that easy. For example, when a child kicks themselves because they can do something perfectly, Think before you say something and learn to react properly because it has a significant effect on your child's psyche. Here are some strategies that can help you teach your child without criticizing or shaming:

•	Stop temporarily. A situation may look serious, but it is probably just your strong emotional response (e.g., being angry, hurt, or afraid). For instance, you feel tired and say to yourself, "Am I asking too much for just some peace for several minutes?" or "How could they behave uncontrollably when I let them play for more time with their computer?"

•	Read a list of questions that you keep in mind and that will help you decide what to do when your child displays difficult behavior. Practice it often, and it will not be so difficult for you! For instance, "In what ways can I teach my child not to do such things in the future?" or "How can I best teach my child to react in situations like this?"

•	Read a list of debriefing questions when you feel less emotional, which helps you solve problems and reduce the occurrence of negative behaviors. For example, "What was the most recent time I talked with my child?" or "What do I need to do to deal with this situation so that my child and I both feel stronger and more confident?"

Finding the right discipline for your child can have a long-lasting effect on their well-being. You and your child are both responsible for not moving back to the same behavioral patterns, although creating new habits is not easy but possible.

A narcissistic parent constantly observes and criticizes their child for everything they do because they have too many expectations and are perfectionists. They never see how well their child does because they think they could do it better. They compare them to themselves or other people similar to them, and therefore children grow up with a lack of self-confidence and mental health issues. A parent-child relationship is very difficult and tense. However, a parent can learn not to be overly critical. They can adapt the necessary parenting styles for the right psychological and physical development of a child.

10

TURNING THINGS AROUND

Parents with narcissistic traits can turn things around with every possible effort to raise their children properly and should seek professional help where needed.

Who to Lean On for Support

When we think about the causes of narcissistic traits in NPD, there is no single one; it involves genetic and environmental factors. Research shows that if a person has a parent with NDP, their chances of developing the disorder are higher in comparison to other personal disorders (Holland, n.d.). Environmental factors can be parents, children, custodians, and other people with whom they communicate. However, an effective treatment can help manage NPD.

Researchers conducted an 18-month study with over 500 children, ages 7 to 12, including their parents, and contacted them four times. They did it to find out the reasons why children develop narcissistic traits. The results showed that a child could become narcissistic when their parents place too much importance on them and differentiate them from other children, but this does not increase their self-esteem. However, those children whose parents showed them love and care were aware of it but did not develop narcissistic traits, but instead strengthened their bond (Kennedy-Moore, 2015).

As a parent who struggles with narcissism, you need to learn the importance of raising your child in a way that will not let them develop the condition while keeping in mind environmental factors. This necessitates the application of all of the strategies discussed in the book. You can help others with your knowledge and actions, and the continuing impact can have an important effect.

Your task is to protect your child's mental health and welfare. Their emotional and mental state should be balanced, and they should be able to accept themselves as they are. They should get appropriate approval for their achievements. You should also teach a child how to react in difficult situations and that it's okay sometimes to make mistakes and to be criticized; the most important thing is the attempt, not the final result. Importantly, show them love.

There are ways that can help you prevent developing narcissistic traits in your child. Love your child with all the good and bad qualities of their character. Consider them your imperfect self. Take them as they are; they don't have to be exceptionally intelligent or a future superstar; they can be ordinary people with modest abilities who make mistakes but still deserve your love.

Be precise when praising. Avoid using general praise like "Well done!" and better use achievement-specific praise like "It's good that you finished your presentation with those questions. It made me consider the progression of this project." Your child is just like you, and you should show that you really appreciate their attempt.

Also, praise what is happening at that moment, not "at all times" or "never," because otherwise, you nullify the effort of the moment. You also diminish the fulfillment of what they did now, even if they may have had difficulties with it in the past or in the future. Say, "Today you cleaned your room perfectly," not, "You always keep your room tidy." Don't generalize their accomplishments and only praise what your child did at the time.

Remember to keep the balance and not to praise them too much; it won't help them become more confident. Because if you do it too often, they will ask for more and for everything you do. In time, those compliments can lose their meaning. Think before you praise your child, and don't do it for nothing because it will do damage to their self-respect. Praise your child, for example, not for every good grade they receive, but for passing a difficult math test. In this way, they will see that it's worth putting in a lot of effort to reap the benefits. They will understand that they are just like anyone else and can make mistakes.

Teach them to treat people equally and not to think of themselves as superior. They should learn not to do to others what they want to do to them. It will aid in the prevention of the development of narcissistic traits. In addition to that, they should learn not to judge someone without trying to understand them. If you do it often, it will help them not think of themselves as superior. They will think about the situations and how those people feel in them.

Of course, there may be a lot more ways to help your child live a happy and normal life. You can really help them to be compassionate and empathetic toward other people. With your assistance, they will see what the limits are, accept their abilities, and see other people as having worth in their lives.

Breaking the Cycle

Parenting a child displaying difficult behavior may be tough. They may think that they have to be exceptionally treated, that they don't care about others' feelings, and that they are arrogant. Also, they very loudly express their frustration if something is not like they want it to be. Therefore, you will need trained support and support from those you know well because you have to consider your mental health, overall well-being, and any stress that you may suffer.

Support will help you feel healthier and free from tension, and thereby you will be able to take care of your child more efficiently. A child will see you as an example, and if they see that you get assistance from someone, they may ask for it too. Asking for support shows that you care about your child and want to keep them special. You will get support in the forms of:

- Practice.

- Counseling and showing compassion and care.

- Giving advice or information.

In most cases, you can get support from various specialists, such as psychologists or medical specialists whose area of specialization is children (e.g., theparentreport.com). Talk to a parenting educator to understand more about the developmental aspects of your child. They will help you set realistic expectations to avoid emotional instability. With the assistance of an educator, it is likely you will discover that there is nothing wrong with your child's development and that you simply need to practice raising them. You can get such assistance from the "One-2-One" program support system:

- Send them an email.

- Call.

- Or send an SMS.

Moreover, you may also get personal and emotional support from typical people, like family members or friends. They can willingly listen and be understanding of your issues and feelings of dissatisfaction, or you can simply spend some good time with them. Together, you will share ideas and thoughts, and maybe they have similar issues or are in situations like you. In such a company, you will speak positively and without judgment, and they will not tell anyone else about it. But avoid talking to people who can make you feel stressed and anxious.

A support system will help you see that your experience as a parent is not so abnormal, and you will not feel isolated either.

In some situations, you may require additional support when you feel that you can't get the one you need. For example, your family members could be far away, or you could be divorced from your child's other parent. For example, if you are a single father, you can find information on Single Dad where they can help you with everyday problems when raising a child. There also may be times when the support network isn't helpful enough to you, for instance, during changes in your life, when you come back to work or change jobs, or when your child begins to go to school (e.g., education.com or Raising Them). You may rethink the support network you ask for help from or look for help from other sources. Support from your family and friends may not be enough, and you may need to get it from other sources:

• Join an online parenting forum and have a chat with other parents (e.g., parentsforum.com).

• Visit your local library, which conducts storytelling sessions for babies and their parents.

• Talk to other parents at preschool playgroups, kindergarten, or simply at the park.

However, if you have a child with a mental disability, you need certain practical assistance for the family and your child. A publicly-funded support worker who works with children who exhibit challenging behavior may be able to assist you. You may find various forms of support online, for example, at My Time. They can offer you parent education programs, groups of people with similar situations and experiences, organize groups for children to play with, and any other groups. Administration and Developmental Disabilities can also provide assistance and information, such as how to integrate a disabled child into society. Family Voices may also be of assistance to children and teenagers with special needs and disabilities.

Nevertheless, don't try to solve the problems on your own because you will feel emotionally exhausted and face other negative outcomes. Having issues with personality disorders is a real deal, and you will not get rid of them without proper treatment. When dealing with narcissism, it becomes difficult to maintain a normal relationship with your child because you feel confused with your thoughts and feelings and can't control your behavior. You may find support for treating mental diseases, for example, at the National Alliance on Mental Illness.

There are ways to get help personally. Treatment depends on which personality disorder you are suffering from. For example, a borderline personality disorder is not easily controlled, but psychologists have done a lot of research on it and found some ways to treat it. One method is dialectical behavior therapy. A session happens one time each week.

It also includes a skills training group that helps people bounce back from the impact of wanting to be treated while also leaving therapy if provoked and being aggressive toward specialists. This therapy is effective because people become aware of their emotions and difficult feelings and can control them. A comparison of traditional psychotherapy and dialectical behavioral therapy reveals that after the therapy sessions, women are less likely to harm themselves or ruin their lives, for example, through gambling (Help for Personality Disorders, 2020).

Another method is also weekly cognitive therapy which gives attention to people's thoughts but not emotions. With the help of a therapist, parents can identify and modify their cognitive distortions about themselves and other people. They interpret and remember their childhood experiences differently during therapy. They come to understand that parents are responsible for such cognitive distortions, for example, when they had to take care of something they weren't capable of, and when they understand it, they make changes. This therapy is effective because a parent has significantly fewer symptoms after a year, and 55% of patients have no symptoms at all and do not need further treatment (Help for Personality Disorders, 2020).

Raising children when a parent is suffering from narcissism is a big problem. It also becomes difficult when a child has a mental disability and their parents face additional problems, not only behavioral. They need to get various types of support, from the closest circle, like family and friends, to the professionals. The most important thing is not to isolate from everyone and try to solve the problems alone, which is not the right decision, but to look for the best possible help.

AFTERWORD

Parenting itself is a very responsible job to do, from when a child is just a baby until they grow up and become independent. It is especially difficult when you deal with narcissism and the responsibility to raise a child becomes unbearable. It is very important how you raise your child—if you are loving and caring enough and take into consideration all of their needs, both physical and psychological. A parent with narcissistic traits may think that all their child does is make them angry and that they are just behaving badly. However, that's not true. They are sending a direct message to their parents. That's how a child craves attention and love from you.

Raising a difficult child requires more understanding and consideration from their parents. When you are struggling with such issues and have narcissistic traits, you can find a lot of necessary information on how to raise a child properly. You can choose from online sources or books. Maybe you already have some information that can help you answer some important questions and take the right steps.

Good sources can help to develop the right mindset, which is crucial in raising a difficult child and not losing your mind! This book, How to Stop Yelling at Your Kids, can point you in the right direction. It can help you feel confident that you have the tools to become a better parent. In addition, it will teach you what to avoid along the way!

Every parent should learn to be patient with their child and communicate with them through actions and words in the best way possible. Because all a child wants from you is to be heard and understood. However, a narcissistic parent may find it difficult to accept the reality that they are not the most important people in the world and struggle with caring for their child's needs. But with practice, you can become selfless.

Of course, there may be many stressful situations when raising a child with difficult behavior, but there are strategies to help you not lose control and manage your anger. Usually, parents both need to share the blame for their actions and words with their children. Everyone must be accountable and responsible for that. Parents should teach their children and teach themselves if they are struggling.

Maintaining balance and not taking complete control of the child is critical to preventing harm to their health and future. A narcissistic parent needs to learn to be less critical of their child's actions because they are the only humans who make mistakes just like themselves. No one is perfect!

Fortunately, there is always help on the way for you as a parent with narcissistic traits and your difficult child. Try to talk with someone reliable and understanding, such as family members or close friends who may have had similar experiences. If you need professional help, you need to refer to appropriate specialists when a child has a mental disability and special needs or when you need help yourself.

FROM
THE AUTHOR

Thank you for taking the time to read my book. My career as a life coach has been so fulfilling to me and if my writing can at least change the lives of just a few people then I think it is absolutely worth it.

Could you do me a favor? Reviews really help out authors get their message out to the world and it would mean a lot to me if you could take a minute to leave feedback on Amazon. The publishing team should leave a QR code below just hover your smartphone's camera over it and the Amazon website should pop up.

Kind regards,
Jamie Williams

REFERENCES

A quote by Kahlil Gibran. (n.d.). Www.goodreads.com. Retrieved November 11, 2022, from https://www.goodreads.com/quotes/115825-your-children-are-not-your-children-they-are-sons-and

Ackerman, C. (2018, July 5). *What is Positive Mindset: 89 Ways to Achieve a Positive Mental Attitude.* PositivePsychology.com. https://positivepsychology.com/positive-mindset/

Active Listening. (2019). *Centers for Disease Control and Prevention.* https://www.cdc.gov/parents/essentials/communication/activelistening.html

Angela. (2017, December 14). *How to Discipline a Child without Criticism And Shame. Parents with Confidence.* https://parentswithconfidence.com/this-is-what-happens-when-you-respond-to-your-child-with-criticism-and-shame/

Anger and anger management for parents. (2020, June 22). *Raising Children Network.* https://raisingchildren.net.au/guides/first-1000-days/looking-after-yourself/anger-management-for-parents

Campbell, L. (2018, July 9). *Children Emotional Health and Overly Critical Parents. Healthline.* https://www.healthline.com/health-news/critical-parenting-harming-kids-emotional-heath#Findings-to-consider

Capriola, P. (2019, August 5). *How Angry Parents Affect A Child: Tips for Raising Healthy Kids. Strategies for Parents.* https://strategiesforparents.com/angry-parents/

Cikanavicius, D. (2020, April 18). *How Narcissists Try to Avoid Responsibility.* Psych Central. https://psychcentral.com/blog/psychology-self/2020/04/narcissists-responsibility#1

Cuncic, A. (2021, November 13). *What Is Narcissistic Rage?* Verywell Mind. https://www.verywellmind.com/what-is-narcissistic-rage-5183744

Devine, M. (2020). *How to Create a Culture of Accountability in Your Home.* Empowering Parents. https://www.empoweringparents.com/article/how-to-create-a-culture-of-accountability-in-your-home/

Drevitch, G. (2021, April 1). *The Hidden Trauma of Neglect in the Narcissistic Family* | Psychology Today. Www.psychologytoday.com. https://www.psychologytoday.com/intl/blog/the-narcissist-in-your-life/202104/the-hidden-trauma-neglect-in-the-narcissistic-family#:~:text=Narcissists%20often%20cultivate%20the%20idea

Ehmke, R. (2016, May 16). *Tips for Communicating With Your Teen. Child Mind Institute;* Child Mind Institute. https://childmind.org/article/tips-communicating-with-teen/

Find Support | National Parent Helpline. (n.d.). Www.nationalparenthelpline.org. https://www.nationalparenthelpline.org/find-support

Good Behavior | Communicating with Your Child | Essentials | Parenting Information | CDC. (2020, June 8). Www.cdc.gov. https://www.cdc.gov/parents/essentials/communication/goodbehavior.html

Greene, L. (2020, August 17). *Proven Ways to Develop A Positive Mindset—and Why It Matters.* Psycom.net - Mental Health Treatment Resource since 1986. https://www.psycom.net/positive-thinking

Hamaker, S. (2015, March 11). *7 ways to nip narcissism in the bud*. Washington Post. https://www.washingtonpost.com/news/parenting/wp/2015/03/11/7-ways-to-nip-narcissism-in-the-bud/

Hammond, C. (2016, May 31). *7 Tactics Narcissists Use to Escape Responsibility* (Scientific Advisory Board, Ed.). Psych Central. https://psychcentral.com/pro/exhausted-woman/2016/05/7-tactics-narcissists-use-to-escape-responsibility#1

Hammond, C. (2018, June 15). *Shame Based Parenting: A Narcissists Specialty* (Scientific Advisory Board, Ed.). Psych Central. https://psychcentral.com/pro/exhausted-woman/2018/06/shame-based-parenting-a-narcissists-specialty#1

Help for personality disorders. (2020). Apa.org. https://www.apa.org/topics/personality-disorders/help

Helping someone with a personality disorder. (2020, January). Www.mind.org.uk. https://www.mind.org.uk/information-support/types-of-mental-health-problems/personality-disorders/for-friends-family/

Holland, M. (n.d.). *Is Narcissism Genetic? Causes & Risk Factors* (K. Fuller, Ed.). Choosing Therapy. https://www.choosingtherapy.com/is-narcissism-genetic/

Home | Communicating with Your Child | Essentials | Parenting Information | CDC. (2020, March 24). Www.cdc.gov. https://www.cdc.gov/parents/essentials/communication/index.html

How Parental Anger Can Affect Children. (2022, March 22). NeuroBalance. https://www.myneurobalance.com/blog/2022/2/27/how-parental-anger-can-affect-children

How to deal with a Selfish or Narcissistic Parent? - Parenting Goal. (2022, August 31). Parenting Goal. https://parentinggoal.com/ways-to-deal-with-a-narcissistic-selfish-parent/

J. Peterson, T. (2022, January 16). *Do Mom and Dad Still Have Differing Parental Roles? |* HealthyPlace. Www.healthyplace.com. https://www.healthyplace.com/parenting/parenting-skills-strategies/do-mom-and-dad-still-have-differing-parental-roles

Javier. (2019, November 13). *Controlling and dominating children: The fear of losing control.* Helping Kids. https://helpingkids.co.uk/controlling-dominating-children/

Johnson, E. B. (2019, April 8). *Growing up Critical: How to recover from an overly critical childhood.* Practical Growth. https://medium.com/practical-growth/how-to-recover-critical-childhood-fd201f826e11

Johnson, E. B. (2020, April 13). *The best ways to stop being so selfish.* Practical Growth. https://medium.com/practical-growth/how-to-stop-being-selfish-e4e012a167b0

Kaminsky, A. (2020, October 22). *Why Criticism and Shame Have No Place in Parenting.* Child Psychology Resources by Dr. Tali Shenfield. https://www.psy-ed.com/wpblog/criticism-shame-parenting/

Kassel, G. (2019, January 30). *11 Signs You're Dating a Narcissist — and How to Get Out.* Healthline; Healthline Media. https://www.healthline.com/health/mental-health/am-i-dating-a-narcissist

Kennedy-Moore, E. (2015, March 10). *How to NOT Raise a Narcissist |* Psychology Today (J. Schrader, Ed.). Www.psychologytoday.com. https://www.psychologytoday.com/intl/blog/growing-friendships/201503/how-not-raise-narcissist

L. Hall, J. (2016, April 16). *A Daughter's Story of One Hell of a Narcissistic Mother -* (G. Drevitch, Ed.). Narcissistfamilyfiles.com. https://narcissistfamilyfiles.com/2016/04/16/a-daughters-story-of-one-hell-of-a-narcissist-mother/

Lo, I. (n.d.). *Controlling Parents Trauma.* Eggshell Therapy and Coaching. https://eggshelltherapy.com/paranoid-controlling-parents/

M. Darcy, A. (2020, July 14). *Narcissistic Parenting - Was This Your Childhood?* (S. Jacobson, Ed.). Harley Therapy™ Blog. https://www.harleytherapy.co.uk/counselling/narcissistic-parenting.htm

Mahoney, D., Rickspoone, L., & C. Hull, J. (2016). Narcissism, Parenting, Complex Trauma: The Emotional Consequences Created for Children by Narcissistic Parents | *The Practitioner Scholar: Journal of the International Trauma Training Institute.* Www.thepractitionerscholar.com, 5(1). https://www.thepractitionerscholar.com/article/view/15841

Main, K. (2013, May 27). *It's not always Sunshine and Roses.* Karen Main. https://karenmain.com.au/its-not-always-sunshine-and-roses/

Mann, D. (2007). *Listening to Your Kids.* WebMD; WebMD. https://www.webmd.com/parenting/features/listening-to-your-kids

Mayo Clinic Staff. (2017, November 18). N*arcissistic personality disorder - Symptoms and causes*. Mayo Clinic. https://www.mayoclinic.org/diseases-conditions/narcissistic-personality-disorder/symptoms-causes/syc-20366662

McBride, K. (2019, January 12). *Lack of Accountability in Narcissists* | Psychology Today (J. Schrader, Ed.). Www.psychologytoday.com. https://www.psychologytoday.com/us/blog/the-legacy-distorted-love/201901/lack-accountability-in-narcissists

Melinda. (2019, March 21). *Narcissistic Personality Disorder*. HelpGuide.org. https://www.helpguide.org/articles/mental-disorders/narcissistic-personality-disorder.htm

Mind Tools Content Team. (n.d.-a). *Developing Personal Accountability*. Www.mindtools.com. https://www.mindtools.com/ami110w/developing-personal-accountability

Mind Tools Content Team. (n.d.-b). *Personal Goal Setting*. Www.mindtools.com. https://www.mindtools.com/a5ykiuq/personal-goal-setting

Mind Tools Content Team. (2009). *Personal Goal Setting – Planning to Live Your Life Your Way*. Mindtools.com. https://www.mindtools.com/page6.html

Morgado, P. (2018, January 18). *How Self Awareness Helps With Problem Solving*. Medium. https://medium.com/@Paki1233/how-self-awareness-helps-with-problem-solving-9906647cf82

Morin, A. (2020, September 17). *How to Handle Out-of-Control Kids* (A.-L. T. Lockhart, Ed.). Verywell Family. https://www.verywellfamily.com/help-my-kids-are-out-of-control-1094959

Morin, A. (2022, June 6). *7 Ways to Give Your Kids Consequences That Really Work* (A.-L. T. Lockhart & R. Scherr, Eds.). Verywell Family. https://www.verywellfamily.com/make-consequences-more-effective-1094774

Namka, L. (n.d.). *Selfishness and Narcissism in Family Relationships*. Lynne Namka. https://lynnenamka.com/relationships/relationships-articles/selfishness-narcissism-family-relationships/

Navilon, G. (2021, August 11). *You were raised by narcissists if you suffer from these 14 things*. Ideapod.com. https://ideapod.com/you-were-raised-by-narcissists-if-you-suffer-from-these-10-things/

Nissim-Matheis, L. (2020, January 9). *Parenting Is Not About Controlling Your Child* (H. Estroff Maranov, Ed.). Psychology Today. https://www.psychologytoday.com/us/blog/special-matters/202001/parenting-is-not-about-controlling-your-child

O'Connor, G. (2022, November 8). *Some Kids Really Are More Challenging—Here's Why and How to Deal*. Parents. https://www.parents.com/toddlers-preschoolers/discipline/some-kids-really-are-more-difficult-heres-why-it-happens-and-how-to-deal/

Parenting and stress - Better Health Channel. (n.d.). Www.betterhealth.vic.gov.au. https://www.betterhealth.vic.gov.au/health/healthyliving/parenting-and-stress

Parents Need Support More Than Ever. (2020, April 30). Parenting Now. https://parentingnow.org/parents-need-support-more-than-ever/

Ph.D, K. M. (2015, September 22). *What Is the Most Overlooked Symptom of Narcissism?* | Psychology Today. Www.psychologytoday.com. https://www.psychologytoday.com/intl/blog/resolution-not-conflict/201509/what-is-the-most-overlooked-symptom-narcissism

Pietro, S. (2016, February 2). *Managing Problem Behavior at Home. Child Mind Institute*; Child Mind Institute. https://childmind.org/article/managing-problem-behavior-at-home/

Psychology Today Staff. (n.d.). *How to Be a Good Parent* | Psychology Today. Www.psychologytoday.com. https://www.psychologytoday.com/us/basics/parenting/how-be-good-parent

Psychology Today Staff (Ed.). (2019). *Narcissism* | Psychology Today. Psychology Today. https://www.psychologytoday.com/us/basics/narcissism

Reid, J. (2020, June 15). *Surviving A Parent's Narcissistic Rage: The Value of the Freeze & Submit Responses*. Jay Reid Psychotherapy. https://jreidtherapy.com/surviving-narcissistic-rage/#:~:text=What%20is%20narcissistic%20rage%3F

Rudkin, A. (2019, July 11). *What Does It Mean To Put Your Children First?* OnlyMums. https://www.onlymums.org/information/what-does-it-mean-to-put-your-children-first

S. Willsey, P. (2020, November 2). *The Powerful Practice of Accepting Reality* (M. Huston, Ed.). Psychology Today. https://www.psychologytoday.com/us/blog/packing-success/202011/the-powerful-practice-accepting-reality

Schmitz, T. (2017, April 30). *Gathering Information* | The Conover Company. The Conover Company. https://www.conovercompany.com/gathering-information/

Sicinski, A. (2010, June 2). *Creating a Life Resource List to Help You Achieve a Goal.* IQ Matrix Blog. https://blog.iqmatrix.com/life-resource-list

Stormshak, E. A., Bierman, K. L., McMahon, R. J., & Lengua, L. J. (2000). Parenting Practices and Child Disruptive Behavior Problems in Early Elementary School. *Journal of Clinical Child Psychology, 29(1),* 17–29. https://www.ncbi.nlm.nih.gov/pmc/articles/PMC2764296/

Support for parents: why it's important and where to get it. (2022, March 28). Raising Children Network. https://raisingchildren.net.au/grown-ups/services-support/about-services-support/support-for-parents-why-its-important

Taibbi, R. (2015, September 23). *Narcissist or Just Self-Centered? 4 Ways to Tell* | Psychology Today (M. Huston, Ed.). Www.psychologytoday.com. https://www.psychologytoday.com/us/blog/fixing-families/201509/narcissist-or-just-self-centered-4-ways-tell

Tedrow, D. (2018, November 29). *No Excuses – Holding Kids Accountable for Their Actions –* Youth First. Youth First. https://youthfirstinc.org/no-excuses-holding-kids-accountable-for-their-actions/

Unicef. (n.d.). *How to communicate effectively with your young child.* Www.unicef.org. https://www.unicef.org/parenting/child-care/9-tips-for-better-communication

Watson, R. (2020, June 8). *Co-Parenting. How To Stop Your Child Becoming a Narcissist.* Rachel Watson Insight. https://www.rachelwatsonbooks.com/blog1/how-to-stop-your-child-becoming-a-narcissist

Why and How to Be a Less Controlling Parent. (2022, March 14). Emilyedlynnphd.com. https://www.emilyedlynnphd.com/blog/why-and-how-to-be-a-less-controlling-parent-to-be-a-less-controlling-parent